Praise for **Shadows**

"A beautifully written memoir from one of the thousands of 'competent imposters' who have been running from pain, confusion and loneliness, the consequences of growing up with the chaos of alcoholism, and its many ramifications within the family. As a young child, Keith lived by the 'don't talk' rule, creating a mask offering him protection from further pain. His skills in survivorship say to the outside world, 'I am doing just fine.' He exhibited many signs of accomplishments and success while living an internal world of numbness and disconnection. A powerful tale of generational trauma, this author's story is a testament of how when we are willing to confront our past, we can find our way to forgiveness, gratitude and self-love."

– Claudia Black, Ph.D., pioneer in the Adult Child Movement and author *of It Will Never Happen to Me* and *Unspoken Legacy*

"Keith Burton's *Shadows of Sobriety* is a raw and brilliantly written memoir of what it's like to grow up in a family gripped by alcoholism that captures the heart of overcoming trauma through faith and resilience. The range of emotions in this book run the gamut from honesty to frailty to strength, and yet, in the end, it is deep faith that makes Burton's message so poignant. There are phrases he uses in this book that will stay with me forever; my favorite is that 'healing is a lifelong journey.' You will be better off for reading *Shadows of Sobriety.*"

– William C. Heyman, Founder, Heyman Associates

"Keith Burton has written the most honest memoir I've ever read, which makes its message universal, inspiring, and ultimately, healing in ways that each of us needs. Pain and panic, rollicking adventure, deeply held faith, and the mysteries of love and family all come together to transform this book into an object of rare beauty. *Shadows Of Sobriety* is a roadmap of resilience I'll reach for any time I fear getting lost. As a bonus, it is beautifully written."

– Billy Shore, author of *The Cathedral Within* and Founder & Executive Chair of Share Our Strength

"*Shadows of Sobriety* is a must-read for anyone who has ever had to cope with the lifelong impact of a dysfunctional family. Keith Burton's raw and incredibly honest path to finding peace is a riveting roller coaster of unexpected twists and turns. This book is beyond inspirational. The author shares valuable life lessons that you, too, can use to overcome seemingly insurmountable hurdles (including alcoholism), excise the demons of your past, and be at peace with the present and what is yet to come."

– Steve Cody, co-author of *The ROI of LOL* and Founder/CEO of Peppercomm

"*Shadows of Sobriety* is a compelling memoir taking readers on Keith Burton's journey from his early childhood in Texas to the heights of his professional career. With a sharp memory and introspection, Burton reveals his vulnerable and tender family memories torn from the pages of time. Those who grew up in an alcoholic household as I did may read his words through tear-stained eyes reflecting what we endured, survived, and for the lucky ones, overcame and healed.

A rich tapestry filled with family triumphs, heartache, cycles of addiction, financial instability, and broken promises wrapped in a mid-century version of the American dream, this book is a springboard that will awaken insights and enrich your understanding of your own journey and help heal the pain of intergenerational trauma."

– Robert Jackman, LCPC, Psychotherapist and
author of *Healing Your Lost Inner Child*

"Among the most powerful gifts we can share are honest stories and lessons learned from our darkest, most painful experiences. Keith Burton's *Shadows of Sobriety* is such a gift. This poetic, beautifully written memoir takes us on Keith's journey from a traumatic childhood—one no one should have to endure, but all too many do. The feelings and challenges he describes are universally human, giving us permission to reflect on our own pasts and heal alongside him.

Shadows of Sobriety offers a convincing testimony that resilience and happiness are possible—especially when guided by love and service, including care for oneself.

I'm thankful that Keith's inspiring life and insights are now available to everyone."

– Heide Gardner, Chief Diversity & Inclusion Officer (retired),
AdAge 100 Most Influential Women in Advertising

"*Shadows of Sobriety* is an intensely poignant story of the author's journey through life experiences, losses, revelations, self-discovery, and recovery. Burton opens his heart and mind for all to see as he wrestles for decades to understand his life, which he aptly describes as a 'quilt of painful memories.' His words are especially powerful (and painful) in passages about his alcoholic father.

Stories of his experiences are moving and reflection-inducing. Burton describes the images and experiences in his book as 'postcards from my journey.' In sharing these rich postcards, he has created a memoir of his past that is a rich legacy. I highly recommend this book for everyone and especially those who may be struggling with family issues and relationships or searching for the Light."

– Bruce K. Berger, Ph.D., author of *Brothers Bound* and
Fragments: The Long Coming Home from Vietnam

"*Shadows of Sobriety* is a deeply profound and unflinchingly honest memoir that invites us into the soul of a man seeking redemption and self-understanding amid the turmoil of addiction. Keith Burton masterfully weaves together the painful threads of his past, sharing not only the scars of a family torn by alcoholism but also the resilience and courage it takes to break free from its grip. His reflections on healing, forgiveness, and self-discovery are a beacon of hope for anyone who has felt the weight of generational trauma. This book is a testament to the power of vulnerability and the enduring strength of the human spirit."

– Jon Harris, EVP, Chief Communications &
Networking Officer, Conagra Brands

Shadows of Sobriety

A Journey of
Self-Discovery
and Healing
a Family Legacy

Shadows of
Sobriety

Keith Burton

Published by Grayson Emmett Press

To contact the author about speaking or ordering books in bulk,
visit www.shadowsofsobriety.com

ISBN (paperback): 979-8-9918502-0-9
ISBN (ebook): 979-8-9918502-1-6

Edited by David Aretha
Book design by Christy Day, ConstellationBookServices.com
Author photo credit: Christy Lee Photography

Library of Congress Control Number: 2024924216

Printed in the United States of America

To my beloved wife, Sue, whose unwavering devotion and patience have been my steady anchor through the darkest times. Your quiet strength has lifted me when I couldn't find my own, and your love has been the constant light guiding me forward.

Contents

Foreword

When I first met Keith Burton in January of 2023 at my therapy office in St. Charles, Illinois, the first characteristic that struck me was his endearing Texas accent and polite Southern nature that immediately reminded me of my now wife, Treslyn, who grew up near Keith's DFW neck of the woods. It's the type of cadence that makes you feel at home.

Over the years, I've found that first impressions are often like meaningful book covers that hardly encompass the entirety of the full manuscript. That's especially true when those first impressions take place in a therapy arena.

The man I've come to know in every moment since that first impression has both moved and inspired me as a clinician, as a Christian, and as a man.

C.S. Lewis once wrote that "to love at all is to be vulnerable." When you read through *Shadows of Sobriety: A Journey of Self-Discovery and Healing a Family Legacy*, you'll come to know an author who undoubtedly leads with his heart and simultaneously explores vulnerability in a way that will be contagious to anyone with a story of childhood adversity or trauma.

As a licensed therapist (and former journalist similar to Keith), part of how I'm trained is to assist clients—particularly men from

Keith's generation—to take their armor off and heal long-trapped and untreated wounds. When Keith entered my office, his armor—comfortable as it had become for him amidst a life of family and career successes—couldn't stay on any longer. The anxiety and panic attacks he'd endured related to health scares with his wife, Sue, thrust him into as vulnerable of a state as any of us can find ourselves in. It is in moments like this that I feel the sincere privilege of working alongside our King in Jesus and a man of Keith's faith foundation to collaborate on a path towards healing.

Many men and women can present with strength when they have their armor on. But courage is best shown when it's off. In Keith, I quickly knew I was working with a client who was ready to go bravely into a daunting emotional surgery—when all the armor shining for decades could no longer coat all the suddenly undisguised bleeding. The first step, and probably most important one, was Keith believing his vulnerabilities to be strengths—instead of weaknesses.

Reading *Shadows of Sobriety*, after witnessing Keith's journey up close as his therapist, has felt like taking in the script of a play that I had the honor of watching live—front row and center.

In this book, you'll play witness to a man facing a traumatic past—one marred by an alcoholic, emotionally unavailable father, and a controlling and overbearing mother. The windows Keith provides into a world of alcoholism and family struggle are, sadly, common. Which is what makes Keith's writing all the more meaningful for those with similar stories. In a world where mental health and addiction are often stigmatized, Keith's story offers comfort and guidance.

Keith quotes Proverbs 31:8-9 in his memoir, which reminds us to "speak up for those who cannot speak for themselves." Not only do I see this book as an honoring to Keith's own inner child, but I see the words of these pages as a playbook to healing for others who have been through similar torment and suffering.

Keith weaves his past and present masterfully, as he takes us into pivotal life junctures in manhood and horrific-yet-normalized experiences in childhood. What most impressed me was the determination and resiliency I saw up close in how Keith faced his past. Where he was robbed of a childhood, I saw Keith use his therapeutic and writing journeys to go back and reclaim that lost part of himself.

I would liken my journey alongside him as a therapist to a boxing coach in the ear of a boxer going into blows for a prize fight. At times where I sensed knockout blows of the past would deplete him, Keith weathered those storms and came back stronger—feeding off the strength of his relationship with Christ and the loving support of his wife. It was clear in this project that Keith was gleaning the lessons learned from his past projects, including the notion of "fighting for things that truly matter," adjacent to his prolific work on *Dax's Case*.

Keith illuminates the key point that our life is so delicately about the choices we make. His choice to engage in deep conversations with his own children and siblings about his life was a powerful way of honoring them with empathy, forgiveness, and love. He used his conversations with them as amplifiers to present his truth in this book, similar to an investigative reporter leaning on his sources for an impactful story.

I'm beyond honored to introduce Keith's memoir to the world. Because it truly is based on a present-day journey that heals a past family legacy, spreading grace and love to others for the future. It's a story of redemption and renewal that has the power to touch hearts and change lives. As readers, you'll come to know Keith as a man of deep faith, unwavering integrity, and boundless compassion.

In our therapy work, developing a counselor-client alliance, I quickly realized Keith and I spoke the same language—both as Christians and trauma survivors. In one of our sessions, I asked Keith what would happen if he went back in a time machine to greet his inner child. Reading his memoir, I like to think of him going back in time and gifting a copy to his younger, trapped self. And for readers, I trust Keith's words can offer similar freedom as a beacon of hope.

Scott Gleeson
Licensed Clinical Professional Counselor
Centennial Counseling Center

Introduction

In the hushed hours before dawn, as the world still sleeps, I often find myself reflecting on the winding path that has led me to this moment. Writing this memoir has been one of the most challenging and enlightening endeavors of my life. It has demanded that I delve deep into the shadows of my past, confront painful truths, and lay bare the realities that have shaped my existence.

For some individuals who grow up in homes with alcoholic parents, childhood is a matter of survival. Each day is a struggle to get through, often requiring them to take care of themselves, their siblings, the home, and even their parents. This was my reality growing up. I became adept at masking the chaos, functioning on the surface while turmoil churned within. Survival mode became second nature, a way to keep going despite the chaos and madness surrounding me.

Amidst the turmoil, there were fleeting moments of beauty and connection that offered reprieve. My journey took me from the quaint suburban streets of Texas to the vibrant culture of Chicago, the towering skyscrapers of New York City, and the serene landscapes of Chartres Cathedral. In these places, whether amidst the hustle and bustle of a city or the quiet contemplation of a historic cathedral, I found glimpses of hope and a deeper understanding of my existence.

I've written this memoir for many reasons, but primarily because I've come to realize that as I grow older, time and energy are finite, and I have a story to tell. As I ponder this journey, I'm reminded of the lines from Andrew Marvell's poem *To His Coy Mistress*: "But at my back I always hear/Time's winged chariot hurrying near." The urgency to document and understand my past grows stronger with each passing day.

This is not just a recounting of events but an exploration of the legacy of alcoholism that has haunted my family. It is a testament to the human spirit's resilience in the face of relentless adversity. It is a story of love, loss, and the struggle for redemption.

I want to make it clear from the outset that this memoir reflects my perspective—the lens through which I experienced the events of my life. It's not my intention to judge or criticize those who shared these experiences with me. Rather, my aim is to offer an honest account of how these moments shaped me and to explore the impact of the choices and circumstances that defined our family. I recognize that others may have different recollections or interpretations, and I respect their truths.

Growing up in a home where dysfunction was the norm, I quickly learned that appearances can be deceiving. My mother, a woman of immense strength yet fragile in her own battles with infidelity, anxiety, and co-dependency, navigated a world that often seemed too harsh for her gentle soul. My father, a looming figure whose alcoholism and volatile moods cast a long shadow, left marks on my heart and mind that I carry to this day. Their struggles became my struggles; their pain became my pain.

There were times in my life, moments of despair when I felt as though I was in a cave of emotional darkness, much like David when he wrote Psalm 13: *"How long, O Lord? Will you forget me forever?"* In these moments, the weight of abandonment and loneliness felt insurmountable. But just as David found solace in his faith, I, too, turned to a higher power, seeking comfort and guidance.

Anxiety has often felt like meditating on problems rather than seeking the One who holds the solution. In Joshua 1:8-9, the command to meditate on God's Word day and night offered a pathway to peace: *"This Book of the Law shall not depart from your mouth, but you shall meditate in it day and night...For then you will make your way prosperous, and then you will have good success."* This spiritual practice became a cornerstone in my journey toward healing and understanding.

I'm not a psychologist or a therapist. I'm a child of an alcoholic who suffered in silence for decades, and now I'm sharing my story in the hopes it will help others. Writing this book has been my way of confronting the stigma and shame that so often accompany addiction and mental illness. It is my hope that by sharing my story, others might find their voices, seek support, and realize they are not alone in their struggles.

Ecclesiastes 3:8 says there is *"a time to love, and a time to hate; a time for war, and a time for peace."* Understanding the season we're living in and unifying behind a clarion call in the arena of life is essential. I'm finally in a season of peace in my life, and it is from this place of tranquility that I reflect on my journey and share my story.

As you turn these pages, I invite you to walk with me through the shadows and into the light. Together, we will uncover the truths that have remained hidden for too long and celebrate the strength that has carried us through.

Welcome to my story. Welcome to *Shadows of Sobriety*.

CHAPTER 1

Shadows of the Night:
Fear's Unspoken Truth

and you will realize
that fear is a welcome
friend at this table
it has been waiting
to tell its story
for such a long time
and for those who choose
to listen, I promise
that it will be
the most wonderful of tales
you will have ever heard
— M. M. van der Reijden, "Winter Magnolia"

Some say that each night, as we drift off to sleep, we silently go insane. As a child, I felt the insanity each night between 10 p.m. and 2 a.m. On his arrival home, my alcoholic father would wake us from a sound sleep by hammering with a closed fist on the side door. Then he would enter the house spewing obscenities at my mother, whose presence triggered a violent combustion within him. Some nights, I woke to the sound of angry cursing and that same closed fist striking a human body, then heard my mother quietly sobbing in the dark.

One night stands out vividly in my memory. It was a warm summer evening, and the cicadas were buzzing outside, their droning chorus like the whining of electrical wires rising and falling. The tension in the air was palpable, a silent prelude to the chaos that was about to unfold. I was lying in bed with my window open, staring at the ceiling, when I heard the familiar thud of my father's fist against the door. His shadow loomed large in the kitchen, and the shouting began. I pulled the covers over my head, but the thin fabric did nothing to muffle the sound. My heart raced as I heard him throwing objects, the crash of breaking glass, and my mother crying.

I would sometimes sneak out of my room and hide behind the door in the hallway, watching the scene unfold with wide, fearful eyes. The raw, primal anger in my father's voice and look of despair on my mother's face—these images are seared into my memory. I felt powerless and terrified, a silent witness to a nightmare that seemed to have no end.

The collective wisdom of a man is worth nothing if he feels nothing. Joyce Rachelle, author of *The Language of Angels*, wrote, "Some scars don't hurt. Some scars are numb. Some scars rid you of the capacity to feel anything ever again." There is a block in my emotions, a heaviness I carry inside. I have two realities: fear and emotional paralysis.

During those turbulent nights, I would retreat into myself, seeking a place where I could feel safe. I would close my eyes and imagine I was somewhere else—a place where the madness couldn't reach me. This coping mechanism helped me survive the chaos, but it also created an emotional block that persists to this day. Sometimes I feel nothing, a numbness that shields me from both pain and joy, from connection. Yet, beneath the surface, something more endures, like potholes hastily patched but not truly repaired. These hidden wounds—concealed, yet unhealed—continue to shape my life in ways I'm still unraveling.

Life exposes our stresses and fractures. Over the years, my private world has been ravaged by personal grief, guilt, shame, disappointment, and a bottomless well of anger. My life is a patchwork quilt of painful memories that enshrouds me. Each square of the quilt has its own meaning, and within these squares, I've lived and died a thousand times.

Looking back, I realize that the scars from my childhood not only run deep but have subtly influenced every aspect of who I am. I've struggled with feelings of inadequacy and a pervasive sense of guilt, as though I were somehow responsible for the turmoil at home. These feelings have permeated my relationships, my career, and my self-esteem. Yet, through these struggles, I've also learned resilience and the crucial importance of confronting difficult truths.

Why is it easy to tell other people's stories but so very hard to tell our own?

I'm a devoted husband, father, grandfather, uncle, and brother. Jesus Christ is at the center of my life. Together with my wife, Sue, we take immense pride in our three adult children, each carving out their own unique paths in life. My career in communications has been fulfilling, allowing me to work at the highest echelons with *Fortune 500* clients and multinational organizations. I've spearheaded strategic initiatives, crafted compelling narratives, and made pivotal decisions that have significantly impacted businesses, shaped corporate cultures, and influenced employees' experiences. My passion extends to mentoring the next generation of educators and professionals, guiding them toward excellence. Yet, amidst these roles, one has profoundly shaped me: being the child of an alcoholic. This experience has overshadowed all others, influencing every facet of my life.

Throughout so much of my life, people haven't really known me because I wouldn't let them. I've been a master of deception: Deceiving those around me. Deceiving others I came to know. And deceiving myself. I've worn a mask so that you—and I—would never know the real me. It would be too painful.

The Human Salvage Factory

Roughly one in five adult Americans lived with an alcoholic while growing up, according to the National Association for Children of Alcoholics. For the tens of millions who are adult children of alcoholics (ACoAs), you know my story.

The world of children of alcoholics is black and white. It's fitting that a photo memorializing a quiet Sunday afternoon with my family was black and white. My two older sisters stood in the foreground, holding their cherished dolls and smiling. My parents stood behind them in a proud, affectionate pose—modeling the iconic '50s family. But someone was missing. In the shadows a few feet away, I stood alone in the front seat of our 1956 Ford Fairlane Victoria.

We're told the image of a disfigured self persists even after a successful surgery, much the same as a phantom limb will continue to feel pain years after an arm or leg has been amputated. While I extracted myself from a dysfunctional childhood a lifetime ago, the phantom memories remain, and I still stand in the shadows.

The pieces of my life flash back like light shimmering on a river. As a young boy, I felt far older, bearing the heavy mantle of the responsible child. My role among the actors on a dark stage was to mediate late-night arguments, stand between the combatants when tensions rose, and bring a semblance of calm to our fractured family. Afterward, I would return to my bed, sleeping fitfully for a few hours before waking for school.

This pattern repeated day after day for years. I thought that if I ignored the fear, humiliation, sadness, and anger, I would be okay. Even now, my siblings, who shared those traumatic experiences, remain silent, as if denying it ever happened.

Psychotherapist Robert Jackman, in *Healing Your Lost Inner Child*, refers to this phenomenon as developing "emotional amnesia" to some of our harsher realities because we instinctively know the deep pain that lies beneath the surface.

I didn't talk about my life with anyone. As author Claudia Black once wrote in her book *It Will Never Happen to Me*, children of alcoholic parents live by three rules: Don't talk. Don't trust. Don't feel.

Dad left home one Sunday afternoon in the '60s to buy a pack of Camels and disappeared for the entire summer. During those long, silent months, our lives shifted in a haze of uncertainty.

Mom called his coworkers, his friends, and even the bookies he hung out with in the underworld of the Dallas mafia, but no one would divulge his whereabouts. It was a bizarre time. Life went on around us, and we didn't tell neighbors or friends anything. When things grew desperate, an uncle nearby loaned Mom $100 for groceries and gas.

When he finally showed up late in the summer, Dad acted as though he had only been away overnight and couldn't understand why everyone was upset with him. He hugged me, his trademark Mennen aftershave and Vitalis hair tonic wafting in the air, and told me, "It's all right—I'm home now..."

The period following his return was one of confusion and mixed emotions. While part of me was relieved, another part was deeply hurt by his casual dismissal of our suffering. In our family, there were never any explanations or apologies. We were expected to accept whatever happened and move on with life. These experiences left deep emotional scars but also taught me resilience and the importance of facing difficult truths head-on.

In the '50s, when Dad was committed to Timberlawn, a Dallas sanitarium, and placed in a straitjacket to treat his alcoholism, it felt as though our family's deepest secrets were on the verge of eruption. The hushed whispers of my mother and grandmother on the glass-louvered back porch, their voices tinged with fear and shame filled the air. I remember vividly the crude Plaster of Paris artwork and colorful beaded bracelets he made in therapy—symbols of his feigned compliance as he sat quietly in his pajamas, slippers, and robe, and puffed on a cigarette. The treatments—Antabuse, electro-shock therapy, and psychotherapy—were battles in a war he seemed determined to lose. He emerged from the sanitarium patients once called "The Human Salvage Factory" not as a man reborn but as a defiant shadow of his former self, his demons more entrenched than ever.

We all paid a price. The collateral damage was heavy and debilitating. There was no way out.

When my oldest sister, Carol, became pregnant at seventeen, she was spirited away to a home for unwed mothers. I loved her; we understood the anguish we experienced together on Rock Creek Drive. When she disappeared one night without even a goodbye, a part of me was taken. The illegitimate son she brought into the world was adopted by my parents and became my beloved brother, Jonathan Kurtis Burton, who for the past twenty-eight years has led the Turning Point Church in Nashville as senior pastor. In Jeremiah 18:4, the Bible tells us that God can take broken things and remake them into something better and more precious. He did that with my brother, who has led many to Christ over his years in the ministry.

Behind our two-street neighborhood lay Duck Creek and Central Park, a sprawling expanse of lush athletic fields, and Garland's municipal swimming pool. Even now, I picture myself on the cool infield grass of a baseball diamond, tearful and ashamed after another week of brutal knockdowns and bitter arguments between my parents. I looked up at the blue Texas skies and asked why I had to endure it.

That's when I first experienced a calmness and the assurance of my Savior. He was there when I needed Him to bring peace and hope. Today, when I need Him most, I sense the Lord's presence and hear his voice in 2 Thessalonians 3:16: *"Now may the Lord of peace himself give you peace at all times in every way. The Lord be with you all."*

"The Best Little Boy in the World"

In telling our stories, hurt people can become healed people. As I reflect on my role in the family, I realize I was always the "good" child. "The best little boy in the world!" Mom would say, her smile wide as she hugged me close. At home and at school, I was the placater, the one who absorbed others' pain to soothe the chaos. Apologizing for things that weren't my fault became second nature, a way to maintain a fragile peace.

Growing up, I never invited friends into my house, a small ranch-style build, because I was too embarrassed. I grew up with three sisters and a brother. After Carol departed, I had to share one of the two bedrooms with my sister Cynthia, while my youngest sister Charlotte and brother Kurtis shared the other. My parents slept on a foldout couch in the den, but only on those rare occasions when they weren't fighting and, later in life, when Dad was home at night and not with his girlfriend and the daughter he fathered at their hidden second home in rural McKinney. The existence of that other family was shrouded in secrecy. I never met them, nor knew any details about their lives—only whispers and fragments that added to the sense of distance and estrangement I felt from my father.

My wife Sue once told me that a mutual friend in Garland had whispered to her, *"No one ever went into Keith's house. It was a mystery!"* She was right.

I lied when telling the truth would have been just as easy. Growing up in a world where lies were the norm, I found it easier to accept my own untruths. As a child, trust was a rare commodity—both truth and trust were elusive or altogether absent. This environment conditioned me to doubt and distrust others, effects that linger even today, more than half a century later.

I dreaded competing in sports and games kids played because, deep down, I felt inferior to my friends, though I never admitted it. They say, "Don't let the perfect drive out the good," but for a perfectionist like me, good was never enough. I became controlling, mastering the art of manipulation, thinking I could avoid pain by repressing my feelings.

When talking with someone, I made a habit of focusing the conversation on the other person, downplaying my story, and not disclosing too much about me. People would praise and thank me for being a caring listener. In truth, I didn't want to be vulnerable. It was control—keeping a stranglehold on how others saw me.

Throughout my career, I've collaborated with business luminaries, leading journalists, professional athletes, prominent entertainers, and renowned scientists, as well as government, military, and political leaders. And yet I felt no connection. Years later, on a predawn flight to New York in my late fifties, at the peak of my career after leading major public relations agencies and their global operations, I came to a sad realization: I had no close friends. I've always kept people at arm's length, rarely letting others know me, see the private me, or experience my true feelings. I was ashamed of my circumstances in life, the madness of my family. I kept it all locked inside.

I hate opening myself up and telling all these pathetic stories. They create in me an emotional quagmire that I can't ever describe. It's wrong for a child to be denied a childhood, to be tormented by pain, fear, shame, disappointment, and sadness. To be a victim. I longed for so very much—but required so very little.

A long time ago, my life stopped being an adventure to be lived. It became a problem to be solved—and that saddens me.

A lifetime of stuffing my emotions. They all piled up with nowhere to go but on top of each other. The emotions remained bottled up until one day when the panic attacks came and destroyed the facade that masked my private despair.

CHAPTER 2

Unbroken Ground

The Big Empty

"The Big Empty," stretching north of Abilene and east of Lubbock, is a vast, seldom-traveled prairie, larger than some states but home to fewer people than many urban zip codes. Its red-dirt farms and sprawling ranches, like the Pitchfork and Matador, seem to exist in another time. It's a kind of place you drive through to get somewhere else—a silent witness to history.

Long-abandoned barns and farmhouses dot the prairie. A breeze ripples across the waters of Miller's Creek Reservoir near Munday. Overhead, armies of stratocumulus clouds parade past swirls of cirrus. There's something mesmerizing about the clouds above the Texas prairie. Traveling across these areas by car for client work in Pampa in the late '80s, I would marvel at how the deep blue skies framed the luminous clouds spiraling above. Sometimes, they appeared low enough to reach up and touch.

It was the vast expanse of The Big Empty that drew my great-great-grandfather, John Henry Martin Burton, Jr., to Texas in 1872. He first settled in Valley View, Cook County, then moved to

Johnson County near Cleburne to a farm on the Nolan River. Later, he lived in Knox and Bell counties.

Grandfather Burton, the eighth generation of our family in America, was born in Calhoun County, Alabama. Tragically, he was orphaned at the tender age of nine months when his mother died in 1848. When he was sixteen, he ran away and joined the Confederate Army in the War Between the States, rendering faithful service to a lost cause before being captured in early 1865. He was held at the brutal Fort Massachusetts Prisoner of War Camp off the coast of Mississippi and was briefly interred at another camp in Vicksburg until the war's end. His half-brother, William D. Burton, was killed in action in Georgia in July 1864 at the age of twenty-four.

Fort Massachusetts, situated on a long, narrow barrier island about ten miles off the coast of Mississippi, between Biloxi and Gulfport, was a place of extreme hardship. Prisoners lived out in the open on a parade ground because there were no buildings or lumber to construct any. "After numerous complaints and requests," one report stated, "some used, dilapidated tents finally arrived along with 500 sets of clothing. The tents were issued to them, but the clothes weren't." By April 1865, the prison reached its all-time high population of 4,365 Confederate prisoners.

The desolate expanse of Ship Island stretched out like a barren wasteland, its sandy shores a stark contrast to the verdant fields of home that Grandfather Burton longed for. Fort Massachusetts, an imposing structure of brick and mortar, stood as a silent sentinel, its walls both a refuge from the harsh elements and a prison that confined his spirit. For Grandfather Burton and his fellow prisoners of war, the isolation on this remote island was a daily reminder of their captivity and the uncertain fate that lay ahead.

Life at Fort Massachusetts was a grueling test of endurance. The relentless heat of the Gulf Coast summer bore down on the prisoners, turning the island into a sweltering oven. With little relief from the oppressive humidity, men struggled to find solace in the sparse shade offered by the structure of the fort. In winter, the island's exposed position made it vulnerable to chilling winds and sudden storms, adding another layer of hardship to their existence.

Sanitation was rudimentary at best, with makeshift latrines and limited access to clean water. The stench of waste mingled with the salty sea air, creating an almost unbearable environment. Diseases such as dysentery and scurvy ran rampant through the camp, claiming lives with grim regularity. Malnutrition weakened the men further, as the meager rations of hardtack, salt pork, and beans did little to sustain them. Fresh vegetables and fruits were rare luxuries, and the lack of these vital nutrients took a visible toll on their health.

Despite these dire conditions, the human spirit proved resilient. Grandfather Burton, like many others, found ways to endure the daily grind. Labor assignments, such as fort maintenance and island upkeep, provided a semblance of routine and a distraction from the constant hunger and illness. These tasks, though arduous, became small acts of defiance against the desolation that threatened to engulf them.

Interactions with the guards varied widely. Some Union soldiers displayed a measure of compassion, sharing their own supplies or turning a blind eye to minor infractions. Others enforced discipline with a strict and unyielding hand, their punishments serving as harsh reminders of the power imbalance. Solitary confinement in the dark cell was a dreaded consequence for those who dared to challenge the rules, a place where time seemed to stretch infinitely, and hope was a distant memory.

Amidst the suffering, moments of camaraderie and solidarity emerged. The prisoners forged bonds that transcended their dire circumstances, finding strength in their shared adversity. Stories, songs, and even makeshift games became lifelines, brief respites from the relentless march of time. In my heart, I'm sure that Grandfather Burton often reminisced about his home and the loved ones he prayed to see again, with these memories serving as beacons of hope in the darkest times.

I've tried to imagine what it would have been like to be seventeen and living this nightmare. Grandfather Burton's time at Fort Massachusetts was a crucible of suffering and resilience. The harsh conditions tested the limits of his endurance, yet they also revealed the depths of his resolve. In the face of unimaginable hardship, he discovered an inner strength that would sustain him through the darkest days of his captivity, a testament to the indomitable human spirit.

When the war finally ended and freedom was restored, Grandfather Burton returned to civilian life, determined to rebuild and find peace in a world no longer torn by conflict. He and Cynthia Pricilla ("Cilla") Pass were married in Fayetteville, Arkansas, on March 23, 1869, four years after his discharge from the Confederate Army. They reared seven boys (and a daughter, Sarah, who died at a very young age), including my great-grandfather, Arthur Thomas (A. T.) Burton.

In Cleburne, Johnson County, Texas, A. T. Burton had five sons. He grew cotton on three hundred acres of the Blacklands Prairie, continuing the family's legacy of hard work and perseverance. My grandfather, A. T. "Pop" Burton, Jr., was one of those five sons, and he was a tailor and later a salesman for Lone Star Gas Company. His wife was Una Virginia "Pete" Stewart. They were married in Cleburne in 1922. Pop and Grandmother Burton were wonderful grandparents, and I regret we didn't spend much time with them growing up for reasons that remain unclear.

My dad, Howard Stewart Burton, was born in Cleburne in 1924. He had a brother, Edgar Neal Burton, born in 1927. Growing up, I was told that Uncle Ed had been struck by an ice cream truck as a young boy, which left him mentally disabled. However, Carol later revealed that while Ed had indeed been hit by a truck, he angrily insisted he was not mentally disabled. He remained bitter for years, believing that the story told by his parents had unfairly limited his life and career. Despite this, he worked at the Resistol Hat Factory in Garland, which was known for producing the Stetson hats worn by President Lyndon B. Johnson.

For Grandfather John Henry Burton, life on the Texas plains in the late 1800s was defined by the harsh realities and technological innovations of the time. Resilience and ingenuity were necessary as settlers battled the elements with tools like John Deere's steel plows, which efficiently cut through the tough soil without clogging. The introduction of water-pumping windmills also transformed agriculture, providing a reliable water source in the dry climate and becoming symbols of hope and perseverance for farming families.

Farming had been a way of life for the Burtons in America since the 1600s, and Grandfather Burton carried that legacy with a deep connection to the land, one that extended beyond traditional methods. He also raised honey bees—a quiet dance with nature that required patience, care, and an understanding of the slow rhythms of life. Beekeeping was not for the faint-hearted. It demanded a delicate balance between the bees' fragile world, the shifting environment, and the sweet reward of honey. As he and his sons carefully tended to their one hundred hives, Grandfather Burton embodied the resilience required to stand firm against nature's unpredictability. This meticulous work reflected his ability to harmonize with the environment, showcasing both diligence and an entrepreneurial spirit as the Burton boys sold their honey in town.

Like beekeeping, which required careful attention to the bees and their natural surroundings, farming on the Texas plains evolved through innovation. The introduction of barbed wire in 1874 revolutionized land management, allowing farmers to protect their crops and livestock from roaming cattle. This invention not only secured property but also helped establish a sense of ownership and stability in an unpredictable world. Communities in Texas were tight-knit, coming together through tough times and sharing their resilience, much like the bees that rely on their colony to thrive.

In the face of these challenges, the people of the Texas plains demonstrated remarkable resilience and adaptability. Their stories of innovation, community, and perseverance are a testament to the indomitable spirit that characterized life in the Lone Star State during the late 1800s and early 1900s. Grandfather Burton, who sported a tightly trimmed white beard in his later years, was described by Lovell Weld Aldrich in his genealogy, *Families of Warriors and Conquerors: Generations of Confidence and Success - The Aldrich and Burton Family Genealogy with Related Lines,* as "a quiet man, about 5 feet, 5 inches tall, with a small build and bald." He was soft-spoken and had a determined attitude in life.

In his final fourteen years, he settled on a modest forty-acre cotton farm between Knox City and Munday. Content with his life, he cherished the land and the loving family who would carry the Burton name forward. His legacy, as author Shannon Adler aptly has said, was carved into hearts, not tombstones, living on through the stories and memories he left behind. Just as his beekeeping reflected resourcefulness and a deep connection to nature, Grandfather Burton's life on the farm exemplified his perseverance, adaptability, and quiet strength.

Upon his passing at seventy-eight on November 14, 1925, the Munday newspaper wrote:

> He was a devout Christian and showed it in his everyday life. He was a member of the Presbyterian Church for many years and for the last 10 years has been a member of the Thorp Methodist church and for five years he was a teacher of Sunday

school class, and all his life he had been an inestimable blessing to the church. He was faithful in attendance, often walking, when for some reason there was no conveyance provided. He was a quiet retiring man, not seeming to take a leading part, but his absence will be keenly felt in the church and in the community. Funeral services were conducted at the Gillespie cemetery on last Sunday afternoon by Rev. Claude B Stovall, and the high esteem in which he was held was shown by the large concourse of friends who gathered there to say their last tribute of respect in this good man, there being more than one hundred cars in the procession from this and adjoining communities. Grandfather Burton is survived by his faithful wife and seven sons, all, of who were present at the bedside when the final summons came.

What a remarkable life John Henry Burton lived. As Aldrich reminds us, Grandfather Burton joined the Confederate Army at sixteen, was captured in battle at seventeen, and endured the harsh conditions of a military prison. After the war, he married at twenty-one in Arkansas and moved to Texas to start anew. Aldrich wrote: "This ancestor, my great-grandfather, raised seven successful sons, farmed the unforgiving Texas plains, and, with quiet conviction, taught Sunday school. At his funeral in the small West Texas town of Munday, more than one hundred vehicles followed his casket—a testament to the life he lived and the countless lives he touched. What John Henry Martin Burton endured in his lifetime is something few of my generation will ever truly comprehend."

Grandfather Burton's story is one of fortitude, resilience, and purpose. From the trials of war to the hardships of farming, he faced challenges that would have broken many. Yet he thrived. His life, rooted in faith, family, and service, left a lasting mark. The long procession of vehicles trailing the hearse bearing his body was a powerful tribute to a man whose strength had earned the deep respect of his community. His legacy speaks to the perseverance that defines our family's history.

For more than one hundred fifty years, the Burtons have left their mark on Texas, building churches, schools, and businesses that thrive today. Those who remained in Cleburne continue to be pillars of the community. Known for their hard work, prudence, and faith, the Burtons have always answered the call to serve. Their lives have mattered.

Grandfather Burton's strength came not only from surviving the harsh Texas plains but also from enduring personal losses—his mother, brother, and daughter, and his time as a prisoner of war. Yet he moved forward, always the quiet leader. The values he instilled—courage, hard work, service, and faith—continue to guide successive generations, leaving a legacy that still shapes our journey today.

A Reckless Descent into the Past

A cloud of dust billowed behind us as we veered off the gravel road onto a dirt driveway leading to the Burton farmhouse in Cleburne. I was seven years old that day, and the memory is etched into my mind as vividly as if it happened yesterday. I still remember the tension in the car, the way Dad gripped the steering wheel, knuckles white, and his eyes fixed ahead with an intensity that made my heart race. What exactly had happened to make him drive the family away so suddenly, and why so fast—so recklessly?

A few hundred yards ahead, I spotted giant earthmovers painted in vibrant shades of green, orange, and yellow, dominating the massive earthen bowl of what would soon become the 1,500-acre reservoir named Lake Pat Cleburne. Their presence was jarring, like an invasion into the world Dad loved. Puffs of smoke billowed from their exhausts as they carved deeply into the land where crops once flourished, and where Hereford cattle had grazed in peaceful, sunlit pastures. Their powerful engines roared like beasts reclaiming the earth, tearing apart the familiar landscape of his childhood with a raw, unstoppable force.

With Dad, there was no middle ground. You were either all the way in or completely out. Consumed by his emotions at seeing the Burton homestead being torn asunder, he was determined to take a closer look. In a split-second decision, he steered the car down a steep embankment with our family in tow. With each bump, we were jolted around in our seats, slamming against the roof, windows, and car doors. Mom screamed out, and my sisters began to cry in fear. The car's wild descent mirrored the turbulence in Dad's heart, a chaos that was all too familiar. Then, with a loud boom that served as a note of finality, the car struck a huge boulder and came to rest on a steep grade with a broken driveshaft. The sudden silence was deafening.

Dad dragged on his cigarette and turned the motor off. He opened the door and stepped out, moving to the front of the car. There he stood at age thirty-five, a solitary figure against the backdrop of a land in upheaval, silently contemplating the magnitude of the day. The earthmovers in the distance seemed to pause in reverence, the dust settling like a shroud over the remnants of the Burton legacy. It was as if time itself held its breath, waiting for his next move.

As he stood, peering into the distance, I remembered the story he told me of the windmill on the Burton farm that stood tall against the vast Texas sky. His grandfather would often spend hours maintaining it, ensuring that a steady water supply was available for the family and their livestock. Dad remembered the creaking sound of the blades turning, a constant reminder of the hard work and determination that defined our family's existence on the plains.

The windmill had been a lifeline, its rhythmic turning a symbol of hope and perseverance. Each groan of the metal and swoosh of the blades cutting through the dry Texas air carried with it the legacy of survival against all odds. Dad's eyes would light up with a mix of pride and nostalgia whenever he spoke of it as if he could still feel the sun beating down on his young shoulders as he watched his grandfather work tirelessly to keep the windmill in motion.

Now, that windmill sat silent and in disrepair. Its once mighty blades hung limp, rust eating away at its joints. The tower, which had once stood as a beacon of resilience, cast a forlorn shadow over the land. The stillness was overwhelming, a stark contrast to the vibrant hum of life that had once filled the air. The desolation mirrored the weight of the years and the burdens carried by each generation of Burtons. What was once a testament to their unyielding spirit now stood as a somber monument to the relentless passage of time and the erosion of dreams.

Dad gazed at the decaying structure, and I could see the pain in his eyes, the silent acknowledgment of all that had been lost. The windmill, like our family, had weathered countless storms but now stood weary and broken. It was a poignant reminder that even the strongest of us can fall, that time spares no one, and that the echoes of our past can linger long after the voices have faded.

Dad's story is one of stark contrasts. He came from a lineage rich with resilience, faith, and community service. Yet, he struggled with demons that led him to break away from these traditions.

What caused him to veer away from the strong values and legacy of the Burton family?

Was he burdened by the immense pressure of living up to the Burton name—a name that had defined and built much of his hometown over generations? The legacy of being from a line of doctors, ranchers, and landowners might have weighed heavily on him, fostering a deep sense of failure and inadequacy.

A. T. Burton, a simple tailor amid a lineage of prominent figures, moved his family seventy-one miles away to Garland in 1939 to seek new opportunities. Dad often reminisced about his love for Cleburne, where his roots ran deep, and where he spent his early childhood surrounded by familiar faces and family history. The move to Garland during his formative high school years puzzled him and left him feeling displaced. It seemed to sever critical ties to his heritage and childhood friends in Cleburne, deepening his feelings of disconnection and loss as if part of his identity had been left behind in the town he cherished.

Perhaps it was also the generational burden of unspoken grief and suppressed emotions, an invisible heirloom passed down through the Burton family over generations. Each generation managed their pain in silence, quietly bearing the weight of their struggles without ever addressing them openly. For Dad, this long-held silence might have eventually erupted into visible turmoil, as the unresolved pain of his ancestors, compounded by his own, finally became too much to contain. The emotional legacy of the Burtons, carried silently through the years, may have found its breaking point in him, manifesting in ways that were both tumultuous and deeply personal.

Growing up, I learned of Dad's service in the Pacific Theater during World War II, an experience that left indelible scars, shaping both his life and ours. His days filled with uncertainty during the war were pivotal in molding his character. Upon returning, he yearned for simplicity, a stark contrast to the burgeoning consumer culture of postwar America, which prized material success—values at odds with the simplicity he cherished. This cultural clash likely intensified his sense of alienation and inadequacy.

In the end, it might not have been a single cause but a complex interplay of childhood trauma, generational burdens, wartime scars, and societal shifts that led to his struggles with alcoholism. Each element contributed to the storm within him, pulling him further from the values and legacy of the Burton family. Reflecting on these layers, I understand that fully grasping Dad's journey requires exploring the intricacies of human behavior, environment, upbringing, and personal choices. His story is not merely about a man who lost his way but about the complex web of influences that shape us all.

CHAPTER 3

Defining "Good"

"What does 'good' look like?"

Alex Thursby peered over his glasses, posing this question in the conference room at the National Bank of Abu Dhabi's (NBAD) headquarters in the United Arab Emirates (UAE). The late-afternoon sky, a pinkish gold, framed the setting sun as it bowed to the Arabian Gulf. "That's what I want to know," Thursby pressed. "What does 'good' look like?"

As CEO of NBAD, the loquacious Thursby was spearheading a strategy to expand from the Gulf into India, the Philippines, Indonesia, Malaysia, and China. His success hinged on engaging his employees to deliver on the strategy. The Australian executive wanted his corporate communications team to adopt best-in-class practices to align employees with the business strategy. Our team was there to create and execute a new strategic direction for employee engagement.

As I pondered his question in silence, memories of my childhood suddenly resurfaced. My mother once showed me what "good" looked like in her life: A photo depicted my parents teaching a Sunday School class at First Methodist Church in 1956. Betty Jean Burton, age twenty-nine, in a bright sundress covered by a cardigan and high heels, played the piano while Howard Burton, age thirty-two, nattily dressed in a checked sports coat, black dress pants, a starched blue dress shirt, a bow tie, and black-and-white wing-tip shoes, led the children in hymns. It was a scene right out of a Norman Rockwell painting.

Mom was a vision of grace, her high cheekbones and expressive brown eyes conveying warmth and wisdom. Her jet-black hair framed her face like a silken waterfall, adding to her timeless elegance. Her lips painted a bold, vibrant red, were full and perfectly shaped. The lipstick added a touch of glamor and sophistication, making her smile all the more striking. She was a captivating storyteller, her impish laugh echoing through our home on good days. Mom would tell stories about herself as "Little Betty," playing as a child on the family farm, living a life filled with the love of the many colorful aunts, uncles, and other relatives who would stay at her home most weekends. She vividly recounted the perils of the Great Depression through which she lived, bringing history to life with her expressive narratives. These tales of resilience and family bonds added depth to her charm and left an indelible mark on our hearts.

Dad epitomized the classic Man in the Gray Flannel Suit, a charismatic blend of Errol Flynn and Tyrone Power. His jet-black hair, piercing gray-green eyes, and million-dollar smile could charm anyone. When he spoke, it was with confidence, charisma, and warmth. Ethical and hardworking, he embodied integrity. Although Dad could be charismatic and well-liked outside the family, our own experiences with him were much more complex. Yet, despite his outward magnetism, Dad rarely revealed much about who he was or what was on his mind. There was an enigmatic quality to him, a quiet reserve that kept his innermost thoughts and feelings shrouded in mystery.

Adventures and Family Traditions

Early in my life, there were, indeed, good times.

The 1950s were a period of exploration and adventure, highlighted by the creation of the new interstate highway system under President Dwight D. Eisenhower. Ever the intrepid traveler, Dad was always up for a road trip. He would enthusiastically load us all into our trusty Ford station wagon or sedan, and off we would go, cruising down the open road toward the Hill Country, Austin, Corpus Christi, or Little Rock. These trips were more than just vacations; they were journeys of discovery filled with laughter, scenic vistas, and the excitement of new experiences. The memories of those road trips, the wind in our hair, and the sense of endless possibilities remain etched in my mind, a testament to my father's adventurous spirit and the joy of family togetherness.

When Dad was near, I was by his side. Weekends were a symphony of charcoal briquets, lighter fluid, and grilled delights as we readied for a backyard feast. This meant a trip to Cliff's Meat Market, where I would scamper inside the giant cooler, the roar of fans blowing frigid air over massive sides of pork and beef that hung overhead. Or we would stop at the filling station on Lavon Highway, where fresh watermelons chilled on giant blocks of ice. We would pick the biggest, juiciest one and break it open over the redwood picnic table, savoring its sweetness in the summer afterglow.

Dad was an avid outdoorsman. He would wake me at 4:30 a.m. on weekends and summer days to head out into the pre-dawn morning for nearby Lake Lavon, where we would fish for hours from the deck of a giant barge or off the side of a boat. He also loved fishing the many tanks and ponds dotting the rural countryside and hunting quail, mourning doves, and wood ducks in the fall. A marksman in the Marine Corps, he could down a bird with a single shotgun blast, then gut it and use the internal organs as bait to pull dozens of crappies from the water. Every outing was an adventure, filled with the thrill of the hunt and the serenity of nature.

My parents loved dining out, taking us to memorable places that became cornerstones of our family's shared experiences. The Highland Park Cafeteria, with its bustling atmosphere and gleaming counters, served home-cooked dishes on classic white plates. The air was filled with the aroma of freshly baked rolls and comfort foods, creating a welcoming and familiar environment that we eagerly anticipated.

At the lively El Chico in Lakewood, we enjoyed zesty Tex-Mex cuisine amid festive decorations and lively chatter. The sizzle of fajitas added to the energy, making each visit a lively and flavorful adventure. The vibrant colors and upbeat music made it a favorite spot for family celebrations.

The cozy Lucas B&B, with its wooden beams and brick walls, offered a nostalgic charm. We often savored their famous chicken-fried steak, a dish that felt like a hug from the inside out. The warm, rustic setting provided a sense of comfort and tradition, reminiscent of a bygone era.

Lastly, the Duck Inn in Lewisville, aptly named for those looking to "duck in" for a cocktail under the radar, provided a serene retreat overlooking Lake Dallas. The menu featured fried fish and legendary hush puppies; each plated with artistic flair. We lingered over each course, enjoying the peaceful surroundings and each other's company. The tranquil lakeside view added a touch of magic to our meals, making them feel special and serene.

These dining outings weren't just about the food; they were rich, sensory experiences. Each place was imbued with its own unique charm and atmosphere, leaving us with cherished memories of family and togetherness.

After each outing, we would pile back into the car for the journey home. I always sat behind Dad, perched up in my seat, eagerly talking into his ear as the wind from his open window whipped across my face. Invariably, he would light a big cigar on the way home, and the rich, smoky aroma mixed with the occasional ash that drifted back to me, creating an indelible sensory memory of those cherished drives.

Then there were the wonderful holidays together with the McCurrys and Jennings on Mom's side of our family.

John Addison and Sue Hulda McCurry, affectionately known as "Pawpaw" and "Mimmie," were more than just my grandparents—they were the bedrock of our family, providing an unwavering foundation of stability and strength. Their confidence and quiet assurance grounded us through life's storms. Mimmie's warmth and Pawpaw's steady presence gave me a sense of security that was unshakable. They embodied the kind of unwavering love and resilience that shaped not only my mother's life but also mine. Their wisdom, kindness, and steadfastness were constants, and their influence has stayed with me long after they've gone, guiding me through my own challenges.

Uncle John and Aunt Bobbie McCurry, always impeccably dressed, brought a touch of wit and elegance to every gathering. Their daughters, Laura and Lisa, and son, John David, added to the lively atmosphere with their charm and poise. They lost John David in a car crash in 1970, and it changed their lives forever. It's been said many times that no parent should ever have to bury their child. The loss of this beloved boy cast a pall over their lives for many years. I think of his smile and laughter every time I visit his grave at Restland Cemetery in Dallas.

The reclusive Great Uncle Howard ("Unk") Jennings, an Army Air Services aviator in the 330th Squadron during The Great War, a green-eyeshade tax accountant, and a hybridizer of a massive iris garden, offered quiet wisdom and a gentle demeanor that was a calming presence. He had survived a gas attack in France but still felt the effects on his lungs many years later.

Uncle Charlie and Aunt Flo Jennings were the life of every gathering, leading sing-alongs and sharing tales of their adventures on "The Cotton

Belt Route" of the St. Louis Southwestern Railway, where Uncle Charlie worked as a conductor for forty years. Aunt Flo, with her vivacious spirit, was a regular at the S&S Tea Room in Neiman-Marcus, downtown Dallas, often dining there with Mom. Their lively stories and infectious enthusiasm brought warmth and joy to our family events.

Uncle Charles and Aunt Mel Long, the adventurous duo, regaled us with tales of their latest escapades, keeping us all on the edge of our seats. Despite losing an eye and a leg in a car-train crash many years before, Charles always allowed me to sit on his lap and knock on his wooden prosthetic leg while I stared in fascination at his glass eye.

Uncle Waylon and Aunt Martha Nelson, with their children—Marty, Mike, Nina, and Nancy in tow—always brought their East Texas charm, youthful energy, and a sense of fun to our gatherings. Once the proud owner of a Cadillac dealership in Atlanta, Texas, Waylon went bankrupt, leaving him broken in both spirit and wealth.

These were the wonderful and colorful relatives we spent Easter, Thanksgiving, and Christmas holidays with. Their vibrant personalities and the warmth they brought to each celebration enriched our lives immeasurably. Whether it was the aroma of Aunt Bobbie's famous pecan pie wafting through the air or the sound of Uncle John's laughter echoing around the room with another bad Aggie joke, these moments were filled with joy and storytelling. Each holiday was a tapestry of shared memories and traditions, with every relative contributing their unique thread to the rich fabric of our family's history.

Translating Values to Strategy

As I snapped back to the present, I realized that my definition of good was deeply rooted in those childhood experiences. It wasn't just about meeting goals or expanding our reach. For me, good meant staying true to our values—integrity, genuine connection, and creating a space where everyone felt appreciated and inspired. Just as the people of the

Kalahari Desert say a story is like the wind—coming from far away, yet deeply felt—my understanding of good was shaped by the lasting impact of those early lessons.

"Alex," I began, "to me, good is about building a culture that reflects those cherished moments from my past—where integrity guides our actions and everyone feels they belong and have a purpose. It's about being open, honest, and fostering an environment where people can grow both personally and professionally."

Thursby nodded, a slight smile playing at the corners of his mouth. "I see. So how do we put that into practice?"

Our team had been preparing for this moment. We suggested a thoughtful approach to employee engagement that combined proven methods with a personal touch. We started with open communication, listening to front-line employees to understand their concerns, and keeping regular, honest conversations going between leadership and staff. This way, everyone could see the bigger picture and their place within it.

We made a point to celebrate all achievements, no matter the size, to lift spirits and show each person's contribution mattered. We offered continuous learning opportunities so employees could develop their skills and advance their careers. To build camaraderie and a sense of belonging, we organized team-building activities and social events.

Recognizing the importance of well-being, we introduced comprehensive wellness programs. This holistic approach made sure we were supporting NBAD's people in every way, creating a positive and supportive workplace.

As we outlined our plan, I could see the change in Thursby's expression. He wasn't just hearing a strategy; he was feeling the intention behind it. We weren't just aiming for growth; we were working to build a legacy of care and excellence that would resonate throughout the organization.

In the months that followed, as we put these ideas into action, we saw a transformation at NBAD. Employees became more engaged, more creative, and more committed to their goals. The expansion into new markets was met with enthusiasm and energy, driven by a team that felt truly connected and valued.

In many ways, the journey to define good in a corporate setting mirrored my own personal journey. It was about honoring the past, embracing the present, and building a future that stayed true to the values I had learned from my parents: integrity, connection, and a relentless pursuit of doing what's right.

Looking back, I realized that those Sunday School classes, family road trips, backyard barbecues, and family gatherings had taught me the essence of good leadership and effective communication. They had shown me that "good" was not just a goal but a way of being—one that could transform not just a company but the lives of everyone within it.

CHAPTER 4

Navigating the Abyss

The year was 1959. We had just returned home from a week-long vacation in Austin. Dad pulled into our driveway and told us to wait in the car while he went to open the front door. The sun had set, casting long shadows across the yard. He disappeared into the house, and minutes stretched into eternity as darkness enveloped the landscape, swallowing him as he ventured into the unknown corners of our sanctuary.

When he emerged, his pallid face betrayed the turmoil within, his voice strained with the burden of unspoken fears.

"Somebody broke into our house," he announced. "I've called the police. Stay in the car until they arrive," he instructed, his words a stark command in the hushed night.

Questions tumbled from Mom's lips; her worry etched in furrowed brows. "What did they take?"

Dad's response was a whisper, laden with the weight of loss. "Everything. My pistol, my rifles and shotguns, jewelry, money…"

When the police arrived, their flashing lights created eerie reflections on the house. Despite their thorough search and questioning, they found no leads, no fingerprints, no clues. It was as if the intruders had vanished into thin air, leaving behind a chilling silence and a lingering sense of unease.

Things were never the same after that night.

Dad returned from the Western Pacific in November 1945. Honorably discharged and decorated as a staff sergeant in the U.S. Marine Corps, where he served as a radio gunner in a squadron of dive bombers, he faced an uncertain future. The officer filing Dad's discharge papers wrote: "Preferences for Additional Training: Natural Gas Engineering if possible. Job Preferences: Undecided. Reason: Will wait and look around."

Before the war, Dad had been a star basketball player and golfer in high school in Garland, poised to receive a scholarship from Oklahoma or Texas A&M when he graduated in 1942. Instead, driven by a sense of duty and adventure in wartime, he left his job as a clerk at the Southern Aircraft Company and enlisted in the Marines in January 1943.

Upon arriving back home, Pawpaw offered Dad a job running the McCurry Supermarket in Garland's popular Duck Creek Shopping Village. He quickly took to his new role and excelled, but tension arose. The McCurrys saw their son, my Uncle John, as the rightful heir to the business. Adding to the tension, Dad was deeply involved in a poor business decision, investing thousands of dollars through Waylon Nelson in rotisserie grills. This venture nearly bankrupted the store when the equipment became entangled in a costly patent dispute.

As if that weren't enough, it was an open secret in Garland that my father was behind the theft of the McCurry Supermarket's safe. In the dead of night, the heavy safe was stolen and later found shattered on a highway, its contents emptied. The next morning, the McCurrys stood at the recovery site, staring at the remains of what had once protected the store's money.

Mimmie, ever the quiet observer of my father's actions, took Carol, Cynthia, and me to the scene. Pointing to the debris, she said, "Now I want you kids to see what Howard probably did." It was no surprise to anyone—Gladys Morgan, who we later learned was Mom's real mother, wrote to her in 1982, admitting she had hired a private investigator who had kept track of their lives. "I have kept up with Howard—way back when he robbed the safe at the McCurry's store," she wrote. From that moment on, Dad was barred from ever setting foot in the store again, his reputation further tarnished by whispers that never quite faded.

Disgraced but undeterred, Dad went to work managing a Cabell's convenience store that Pawpaw built across from the supermarket. Faced with the financial disasters at the supermarket, Pawpaw created the convenience store as a lifeline, selling bread, milk, and other essentials to quickly generate cash. Together, they embraced the challenge, with Dad growing a loyal base of customers and Pawpaw ensuring the store was a success, determined to recover from the setbacks.

The Burton family continued to grow with two daughters, Carol and Cynthia, and a son—me—born in July 1954. One day, as Dad tended his customers, a man drove up in a shiny new Ford sedan to buy cigarettes. James Milton "Red" Bankston, a colorful character who had acquired the coveted Ford dealership in Garland, was looking for a cracker-jack salesman.

"You must be Howard Burton," Red said, extending his hand. "I've heard you're the best salesman around."

Dad looked up, a smile spreading across his face. "That's what they say. How can I help you today?"

Bankston's booming voice and infectious laugh filled the store. "I need a salesman for my new dealership. What do you say? Interested in a change?" It didn't take Dad long to accept the offer.

He thrived in this new role, transforming from a store clerk into a top-tier salesman, a role that brought him great success and a deep sense of fulfillment.

Descent into Darkness

Alcohol doesn't change who you are; it reveals who you are. During this period, Dad's behavior plunged into a sinister abyss.

He began drinking heavily, often losing himself in alcohol to cope with his inner turmoil and unresolved pain. This reliance on alcohol was soon compounded by an obsession with gambling. He spent countless hours at backroom card tables at the Glen Lakes Country Club or in one of many flophouse apartments in seedy Dallas neighborhoods, risking money he couldn't afford to lose. He frequently placed bets on college and professional games, hoping for a win that rarely came. This combination of heavy drinking and gambling created a cycle of addiction and financial instability that profoundly affected his life and ours.

Amidst this turmoil, Dad found himself ensnared in the Dallas underworld. He began spending time with a sinister crowd, frequenting The Egyptian Lounge Restaurant, a dimly lit establishment with an air of mystery and danger. Owned by the Campisi family, the restaurant was more than just a place to dine; it was a hub for some of Dallas's most infamous figures. There, he mingled with reputed mobsters Joseph Civello and Jack Ruby—the latter infamously linked to the JFK assassination as Lee Harvey Oswald's killer. Dad also became a regular at Ruby's Carousel Club, a downtown strip joint, where he met Candy Barr. He was utterly smitten by Barr, the renowned stripper and burlesque dancer of the late '50s and '60s. Famous for her performances in Dallas and later in Las Vegas, as well as her high-profile connections and tumultuous personal life, she captivated many with her beauty and charisma, leaving a lasting impression on everyone, including my father.

As Dad's fascination with the underworld deepened, so too did his involvement in risky behaviors and secret affairs with women linked to these notorious figures. This secrecy further strained his relationship with Mom and destabilized our family, adding layers of tension and mistrust. All light produces some shadows, and Dad's newfound lifestyle cast long, dark ones over our family.

Despite his newfound success, the shadow of the Dallas underworld loomed large. Then, one fateful day, we returned from vacation to find our home violated and our sense of security shattered. Although we never knew for certain if the burglary was tied to Dad's underworld connections, it marked a turning point—the day the music died on Rock Creek Drive.

As Dad's drinking spiraled out of control, he became increasingly unpredictable and dangerous, often sinking into a daily stupor that terrified us all. Early one morning, he went off the deep end. After an all-night bender, he ran into our backyard and climbed up on our child's slide. He sat there, rocking back and forth, not saying a word. Mom had to climb up, take his hand, and pull him back down to the ground. My sisters and I were shocked to see Mom leading him into the house. This incident was a glaring sign of how far he had fallen.

He stopped paying our bills, and the mortgage company soon threatened foreclosure until our grandmother stepped in to pay off the balance. Mom was forced to scrimp and pull together what little cash she had to pay the most delinquent bills and buy groceries. We were living hand-to-mouth.

It became common to see utility workers in our yard with a large pipe wrench, shutting off the gas or water for non-payment. One morning, I walked outside to find our car missing from the driveway. Mom told me it had been stolen overnight. In truth, the car had been repossessed while the neighbors watched it being towed away. Things got so bad that even the newspaper delivery boy, angry that he had not been paid for weeks, tore the screen door off its hinges. He was our next-door neighbor, and the news of our financial plight quickly spread through our small enclave of homes.

Alarmed by the man he had become, Mom reached her breaking point. One afternoon, she drove to the Ford dealership to see Bankston. "Red, I need your help," she said, her voice shaking. "Howard is out of control. We need to get him into treatment."

Bankston nodded seriously. "I'll do whatever it takes. Let me make some calls for you."

Together, they made the difficult decision to commit Dad to Timberlawn, the psychiatric hospital known for treating severe cases of addiction. With Bankston's support, Dad was admitted and underwent six weeks of intensive treatment, a crucial step in confronting the demons that had taken over his life.

Dad played the part well at Timberlawn, convincing the doctors and staff with a performance of progress and cooperative spirit. But beneath the facade, he was counting the days until his release. Dad always knew the right things to say and how to appear sincere, all the while plotting his escape from the confines of treatment.

When he finally returned home, there was a brief period where things seemed better. He was more present, more attentive. We dared to hope that perhaps this time, he had truly changed. Life began to settle into a fragile semblance of normalcy.

Yet, Mom remained on edge, her instincts honed by years of experience. She watched him closely, her eyes tracking his every move, her heart bracing for the inevitable.

"Howard, are you *really* okay?" Mom asked, her voice full of hope and fear. She searched his eyes for any sign of the darkness that had previously consumed him.

"I'm fine," Dad replied, though his voice was unconvincing.

But the tension in our home was palpable. It simmered just beneath the surface, a constant reminder that our peace was built on shaky ground. We all sensed it, that uneasy feeling that this calm was only temporary, a fleeting illusion before the next storm.

The facade of improvement cracked more with each passing day. We knew it was only a matter of time before the darkness would reemerge, threatening to engulf us all once again.

CHAPTER 5

A Cold Wind Blows

January 8, 1962, was a windy winter day in Dallas, with blue skies and fifty-degree temperatures. The brisk air carried a sense of foreboding that contrasted sharply with the clear sky above. Sixty-one-year-old G.E. Hall was driving from downtown to his North Dallas home, his mind likely on the day's business activities and his evening plans.

As Hall navigated the quiet streets of a residential area, his car was suddenly overtaken by another vehicle and forced off the road. He barely had time to register what was happening before two armed men emerged, their guns glinting menacingly in the sunlight.

Hall gripped the steering wheel tighter, watching in the rearview mirror as the men, hats pulled low, approached with deliberate steps. His heart thudded loudly in his chest, each beat echoing the cold dread seeping into his bones. The situation escalated rapidly, each second stretching into an eternity.

"Get out of the car!" one of the men barked, his voice harsh and commanding. Hall's heart pounded, but he stayed rooted to his seat, instinctively knowing that any sudden movement could be his last.

Hall's thoughts raced. *Who are these people? What do they want with me?* Panic threatened to overwhelm him, but he forced himself to stay calm. He had to think clearly, to find a way out of this. The faces of his family flashed before his eyes—his wife, Christine, and their children. He couldn't let anything happen to him; they needed him.

The men reached the car, guns aimed squarely at Hall. The tension in the air was thick, a dangerous cocktail of fear and aggression. Hall's eyes darted between the two assailants, searching for any sign of mercy or hesitation, but he found none.

One of the men yanked the car door open and wrenched Hall from his seat, the barrel of his gun aimed at Hall's head. "Hi, Uncle! Let's go for a little drive!" Hall's eyes widened in shock as he recognized his nephew, *Red Bankston*. A wave of betrayal and confusion crashed over him. *This was family!*

"*Red, what the hell is going on here?*" Hall demanded, trying to mask his fear with anger. The cold wind cut through his coat, amplifying his vulnerability.

"You'll find out," Bankston replied coldly. "Let's go."

Hall glanced around and saw Howard Burton, another familiar face, opening the trunk of the car. They manhandled Hall into the trunk, slammed it shut, and then drove off at a high speed. *This can't be happening*, Hall thought. *How did it come to this?* His mind was a whirlwind of memories—Christmases, family gatherings, moments shared with the nephew who was now threatening to harm him.

The Dallas Police report aired three days later by WBAP-TV, the Dallas-Fort Worth NBC affiliate, detailed the harrowing events that followed. The men drove to North Dallas County, near Addison, before stopping. Hall was dragged from the trunk and savagely beaten. Bankston fired three shots in his direction, all purposely missing their mark, but the message was clear.

"You're going to pay me what you owe me, Uncle," Bankston hissed. "No more waiting! One and a half million, or I'll drag you behind this car until there's nothing left."

Hall's mind reeled. *The lawsuit!* he realized. *This is about the lawsuit!* Bankston had brought a civil action against his uncle in 1958 and was still awaiting settlement four years later.

Hall, who had made millions in the oil business, was no stranger to courtrooms and litigation. Whether it was fighting to reclaim the sunk costs of dry holes from wildcat wells, fattening a tax write-off to cover a bad gambling debt with Dallas mobster and illegal gambling czar Benny Binion, or other challenges that came his way, he was always prepared.

Police reports indicate that Bankston and Dad eventually released Hall and delivered him without further harm to his sister's home in Dallas. They were arrested two days later on kidnapping and extortion charges, and they bonded out within an hour.

Five days later, the three men appeared for a hearing before Justice of the Peace W.E. Richburg. During the hearing, Bankston and Dad signed peace bonds in the amounts of $25,000 and $5,000, respectively, barring them from any future contact with Hall. The terms of the settlement were never disclosed. All charges were dropped, but the scars remained.

Red Bankston was never the same. After Dad left Bankston Motor, Inc., to work as a salesman at Friendly Chevrolet in Dallas, putting his brush with the law behind him, Red remained under scrutiny. Following the assassination of JFK on November 22, 1963, the FBI began investigating reports that Red had sold a car to James Henry Dolan, who some alleged was one of the president's assassins. They sought to understand Bankston's connections to Dolan and what he might have known about Dolan's occupation and criminal activities.

Bankston never received the hoped-for judgment from Hall. Bordering on bankruptcy, he sold the Garland Ford dealership to Courtesy Motors Corp of Englewood and Denver, Colorado.

On May 15, 1964, police arrived at Bankston's Garland home after receiving a call from his mother. They found a .357 Magnum pistol near his body, with a wound indicating the weapon had been aimed at his heart. In a twist of fate, the investigation and ruling on Bankston's death fell to Justice of the Peace Theron Ward, a former classmate of Mom's and the same magistrate who would later face controversy for allowing JFK's body to be removed from Parkland Hospital and transported back to Washington, D.C.

Dad moved on with his life. That year, he was honored with the Dallas Salesmanship Club's highest award for selling a record number of Chevrolets, a testament to his resilience and dedication. He never forgot the day Red Bankston stopped at the Cabell's' store on Rock Creek and said, "I've heard you're the best salesman around." Those words had lingered with him, a challenge he finally proved true. This achievement not only solidified Dad's reputation but also brought a measure of redemption from his tumultuous past.

The award ceremony, held at the prestigious Dallas Country Club, was a grand affair. As Dad stepped up to receive the plaque, the applause from his peers was thunderous, a chorus of validation he had longed for. Each clap seemed to echo the struggles and triumphs of his journey—from the countless hours spent on the dealership floor to the personal battles he fought behind closed doors.

Bankston's words were more than a compliment; they were a lifeline thrown to a man adrift. Dad often recounted that moment—the crisp morning air, the scent of fresh pastries wafting from the store, and Red's confident stride as he approached him. "You've got something special, kid," Red had said, patting him on the back. "Don't ever let anyone tell you different."

Red's influence on my father ran deeper than a simple compliment. He was the embodiment of my father's aspirations. Every venture they undertook was not just a business opportunity but a chance to chase the dreams they had spun in their brief years together. Red's enthusiasm and unwavering belief in their potential fueled my father's ambitions, turning their shared dreams into a beacon of hope in an often uncertain world.

On a psychological level, Red served as Dad's emotional anchor. Through the highs and lows of their endeavors, Red's companionship provided a sense of stability. My father could always count on Red to share his burdens, validate his struggles, and celebrate his successes. This emotional support was crucial in a world where Dad often felt isolated by his responsibilities and failures.

As the years passed and their paths diverged, Red became a spectral figure in Dad's life—the ghost of what might have been. Every missed opportunity and unrealized dream was a haunting reminder of the potential that was never fulfilled. Red's memory lingered, casting a long shadow over Dad's achievements and failures alike. Despite the weight of these unfulfilled dreams, Red also served as a catalyst for Dad's perseverance. The part of him that resonated with Red's unyielding spirit kept pushing forward, striving for that elusive success.

In essence, Red Bankston was a pivotal figure in shaping my father's psychological landscape, influencing his aspirations, self-worth, and the relentless pursuit of a dream that remained just out of reach. Through Red, Dad's life was a poignant blend of hope and regret, determination and doubt, forever chasing the shadows of unfulfilled potential. Red's legacy was complex, intertwining camaraderie with a constant sense of what was missing. He represented both the joy of shared dreams and the pain of unachieved goals, leaving an indelible mark on my father's heart and mind.

That recognition, years later, was more than just an award. It was a vindication of Dad's potential, a beacon that guided him through the darkest times. It marked the culmination of years of perseverance and the beginning of a new chapter where he could finally leave behind the shadows of his past.

CHAPTER 6

Beneath the Surface

I t was the summer of 1984. I had just arrived home in North Garland, physically spent after a long day at work and a grueling commute from downtown Dallas. As I tried to unwind with Sue and our three young children, the phone's shrill ring shattered the momentary calm. I answered, the weariness in my voice unmistakable, but a knot of uneasiness tightened in my chest as soon as I heard her voice.

"Are you home now?" my mother's voice, upbeat but urgent, came through the line.

"Yes, Mom. What's up?" I replied.

"I'm coming over," she said. "I have something to show you."

Minutes later, a car horn sounded. Peering through the front window, I saw Mom waving from her car. As I went out to greet her, she rolled down the window, letting a rush of cool air and the scent of her trademark White Rain hair spray mix with the stifling summer heat.

"Do you have time to drive with me? I want to show you something," she asked, her eyes holding a secret I could feel in my bones. "I want you to drive," she added, sliding over into the passenger seat. I waved to Sue, standing in the front door with the kids, and told her I would return shortly.

We drove west for a short distance, turned onto Jupiter Road, and then headed north for a mile, passing Campbell Road. The silence between us was comfortable, filled with anticipation. Mom's fingers tapped lightly on her knee, a habit she had when she was nervous or excited.

"There—turn there at the church!" Mom directed. On my right was a historic Baptist church and the Big Springs Cemetery, established in 1868, its weathered headstones bearing silent witness to the passage of time. I turned into the driveway, the crunch of tires on gravel the only sound in the serene, somber surroundings.

We exited the car and Mom tightly locked her arm in mine. "Let's walk beyond that stand of cedars up ahead," she directed. We passed several headstones marking gravesites of the fallen, long buried in the now-closed cemetery. She pointed toward a cluster of old trees and a larger gated entrance. "Over there," she said softly. We walked among the tombstones, each telling its own story of a life lived.

As we walked, my thoughts wandered to Mom's early life in Dallas. Born Betty Jane Morgan, she was orphaned at a young age. Taken in by Mimmie and Pawpaw, she grew up as Betty Jean McCurry, enjoying a good life in a middle-class family during the Great Depression. Like Mom, her brother John was also orphaned and adopted by the McCurrys, who provided both children with a loving, stable Christian home that shaped their values and upbringing. "Mom, why did you bring me here?" I asked, curiosity and concern mixing in my voice.

"I wanted to share something important with you, something about our family," she replied, her tone serious yet tender.

Pawpaw was a bookkeeper for Swift and Company and Triway Produce in Dallas, and Mimmie was a former teacher and a housewife. They lived off Gaston Avenue in a one-story frame house with all the modern conveniences. Remarkably, the McCurrys were a two-car family, which was exceptional during the Depression. Despite this, Mom mostly transited around Dallas using buses, streetcars, and Interurbans. She attended nearby Rusk Elementary and loved her roller skates and playing jacks, Monopoly, and Red Rover. Shirley Temple and Andy Hardy movies were her favorites.

The McCurrys were active in their church and spent much of their time with relatives or on their farm in Garland, where they grew onions as a crop they sold to area grocers. Favored vacation spots included Austin, San Antonio, the Hill Country, Galveston, and Corpus Christi.

The McCurrys moved twice during Mom's childhood—first from their Gaston Avenue address to another house near downtown Dallas, and later to Degge Circle in Garland when Mom was fourteen. It was there that she met Dad, when they began attending Garland High School. Dad enlisted in the Marine Corps on January 9, 1943. They were married in a traditional double ring ceremony at the First Presbyterian Church on June 13, 1943, while Dad was stationed in Oklahoma.

We always knew Mom was adopted, but her heritage was never questioned—except by Dad. In his worst, drunken rages, he hurled vile names at Mom and cruelly reminded her that she had been abandoned by her natural mother. I can still see the pain in Mom's eyes as he cursed and condemned her, sometimes for hours.

Dad's insults were particularly cruel, cutting deep into her sense of identity. He would sneer, "No wonder your own mother didn't want you," and the words would hang in the air like a dark cloud, suffocating us all. Each accusation seemed to erode a piece of her spirit, and I could almost hear the sound of her heart breaking.

Those nights were the worst. The house would be filled with the stench of Canadian Club whisky and the echo of Dad's venomous tirades. The sharp scent of alcohol seemed to seep into the walls, mingling with the faint mustiness of old wood and dust. Mom would sit silently in the den, crying, her eyes cast down as if trying to disappear into the dark, grooved patterns of the wainscoting. Her shoulders would shake with silent sobs, each tear a testament to the barrage of insults she endured.

I often sat in the hallway, straining to be invisible, the weight of their pain pressing down on me. The sound of the giant attic fan whirring above me only amplified the tension in the air; its relentless drone a constant reminder of the turmoil within our home. My heart would race, a mixture of dread and helplessness coursing through me. I was torn between the instinct to protect her and the fear of becoming his next target.

The fear was paralyzing. I would press my back against the cold wall, trying to blend into the shadows, wishing I could vanish altogether. Each shout, each cruel word, felt like a physical blow, reverberating through the house and leaving a trail of invisible scars. I would clench my fists, nails digging into my palms, as if the pain could somehow ground me, give me the strength to endure the nightmare unfolding before me.

Mom's resilience was both her shield and her prison. She rarely fought back, choosing instead to absorb the blows, perhaps believing that her silence would somehow protect us from further harm. But her silence spoke volumes. It was in the tight set of her jaw, the way her hands would tremble ever so slightly as she gripped the couch, and the haunted look that lingered in her eyes long after Dad had fallen asleep in his chair.

I remember one particular night vividly. Dad had been drinking heavily, more so than usual. His words were slurred but no less sharp, each one a dagger aimed at Mom's very being. "You're nothing but a worthless bitch," he spat, the words dripping with disdain. Mom flinched, but she didn't cry. Instead, she stared at a spot on the wall, her mind seemingly miles away, perhaps clinging to memories of a time before the pain, before the betrayal.

The aftermath of these tirades was equally painful. The next morning, the house would be eerily quiet, as if holding its breath, waiting for the next storm. Mom would go about her chores with a mechanical efficiency, her face a mask of stoic determination. But I knew the scars were there, hidden beneath the surface, festering wounds that never quite healed.

In those moments, I grappled with a mix of emotions—anger at Dad for his cruelty, sorrow for Mom's suffering, and a burning desire to understand why she stayed. It wasn't until much later in life that I began to comprehend the complexities of her love and her fears, the intricate web of loyalty and dependency that kept her bound to him despite the pain.

Walking in the cemetery, Mom suddenly halted and pulled back on my arm. "Here it is," she said, looking down. *"I wanted you to see where your grandfather is buried."*

Her voice wavered with emotion as we stood in silence, the weight of history and family secrets pressing down on us. The gravestone, weathered by time, bore the name Vivian C. Morgan, born in 1903, died in 1968. My mind was racing, trying to process the significance of this moment. Then, with a gravity that seemed to echo through the silent cemetery, Mom looked at me and said, *"He's a Comanche Indian. His great-grandfather was Quanah Parker. You have Indian blood…"*

Quanah Parker was the last and greatest chief of the Comanche tribe and among the first leaders of the Native American church movement. He was lionized in S. C. Gwynne's *Empire of the Summer Moon.*

I was stunned into silence. The air seemed to thicken around us, every detail of the cemetery sharpening in my vision. The stories and whispers of the past converged in that instant, and I felt a profound connection to the legacy that shaped our lives. The revelation was like a key turning in a long-forgotten lock, opening a door to a deeper understanding of our family's roots and the cultural heritage that flowed through our veins.

I thought about how Mom's journey from being an orphan to becoming part of a loving family had shaped her. The McCurrys had given her a sense of belonging and security, something she had tried to pass on to us despite the challenges. This moment at the cemetery was more than just a visit to a grave—it was a testament to the legacy and history that defined our family.

CHAPTER 7

A Legacy of Secrets and Sacrifice

As the USS *Copahee* steamed from Guam to San Francisco in November 1945, Dad found his way to the flight deck of the aircraft carrier that had ferried him to Ulithi Atoll earlier in the year and was now taking him home as part of Operation Magic Carpet. The sunrise over the Pacific was majestic, filling the ocean sky with a golden warmth that stretched across the horizon. The sky transitioned from deep navy to vibrant hues of orange and pink, casting a serene glow on the restless ocean below.

He lit a cigarette, the lighter's flicker briefly illuminating his face. The first puff of smoke curled around him before the wind whisked it away as waves crashed against the hull. The salty spray mingled with the morning mist, creating a fine layer of moisture on his skin. The *Copahee*'s signal flags snapped to attention in the growing gale, their bright colors contrasting sharply against the expansive blue.

As he stood there, memories of his journey across the Pacific flooded back. The vastness of the ocean was overwhelming, especially for a small-town boy from Texas. Traveling by aircraft carrier, Dad was struck by the enormity of it all—the endless miles of open water. He marveled at the bravery of the original island navigators who journeyed in hand-carved canoes between secluded islets scattered throughout this immense expanse. He was told the Micronesian navigators were among the finest seafarers in the world.

Ulithi Atoll was a tiny speck in the Pacific, over seven thousand miles away from California, and yet it had become a pivotal point in the war effort. For Dad, the atoll symbolized both the immense scope of the conflict and his small part in it.

Dad pulled from his pocket a letter he had been carrying for months, its edges worn and creased from constant handling. He had read it countless times, studying its contents in quiet moments between sorties against the Japanese forces on nearby Yap Island or after patrolling the waters off Ulithi, guarding against enemy submarine attacks on any one of the hundreds of supply vessels anchored offshore. The paper was thin and fragile, with ink smudges where his fingers had traced the words over and over—particularly the final sentence, which, strangely, was penned in a different color of ink, as though it had been added deliberately after much thought.

As the bow of the carrier lifted and fell in unison with the shifting waves, he began reading again. The words were familiar, yet each reading brought a new wave of emotions. The ship's rhythmic motion was a stark contrast to the storm of feelings within him. The letter was from his wife, Betty, who, despite being a beacon of love and hope amid the chaos of war, had also become a source of mystery and unanswered questions.

Garland, Texas—June 13, 1945
My Darling Husband,

This card doesn't even begin to say all the things I feel and my deep, eternal love for you. The past two years of our lives together have been the happiest and most beautiful. You have given me everything I could want—most importantly, your

love, devotion, understanding, and faith in me. **And giving
me your baby has meant everything to me.**
    All of My Love Always,
    Your Wife, Betty

He could almost hear Mom's voice, soft and reassuring, as he read
the words. The memories of home, of simpler times, mingled with the
harsh realities of war. Each sentence was a reminder of what he had
left behind and what he hoped to return to. The letter was a lifeline,
a connection to a world that seemed distant and almost unreal amid
the vast expanse of the Pacific.

Dad's thoughts drifted to the past, to the beginning of his journey
in the Marines. He had enlisted and quickly shipped out to Norman,
Oklahoma, for basic training. After basic, he was transferred to Naval
Air Gunners School in Purcell, Oklahoma, in July 1943. By April 1944,
he was stationed at El Toro in California, preparing for deployment to
Ulithi, a top-secret base in the Pacific, in March 1945 through the end
of the war. As a radio gunner in Marine Scout Bomber Squadron 245,
he flew countless training and combat missions aboard the Douglas
SBD-5 Dauntless dive bomber on carrier- and land-based operations.

Captured by the United States in September 1944, Ulithi Atoll
became a key logistics and staging area for the U.S. Navy during the
war. It provided a safe harbor for hundreds of ships, including aircraft
carriers, battleships, cruisers, destroyers, and supply vessels. The lagoon
could shelter up to seven hundred ships at a time, making it one of the
largest anchorages of the war.

Ulithi supported major operations such as the invasions of Iwo
Jima and Okinawa, serving as a repair and resupply point that enabled
the fleet to remain operational without returning to distant bases.
Equipped with floating dry docks and various service ships, the base
allowed for extensive maintenance and repairs on-site. The atoll also

hosted airstrips and seaplane bases, crucial for reconnaissance and anti-submarine patrols.

At its peak during World War II, Ulithi hosted a staggering number of military personnel and ships. Approximately twenty thousand troops were stationed there, with a significant portion of them using Mog Mog Island as a recreation hub. This temporary population made the atoll one of the largest naval bases in the Pacific Theater.

The island provided facilities for rest and recreation, including sports fields, movie theaters, and refreshment stands, which were crucial for maintaining morale and combat readiness among the troops. Mog Mog Island was also notable for its free-flowing alcohol, which became a significant part of the off-duty experience for many soldiers. This environment, while offering a much-needed respite from the harsh realities of war, also introduced some to habits that would later haunt them. It was here that Dad admitted he began drinking heavily, a habit that would have lasting implications on his life and our family.

The memories of those early days, filled with intense training and anticipation, seemed like a lifetime ago. Now, as the *Copahee* sailed steadily toward home, he felt the weight of those years—the experiences that had shaped him and the new challenges that lay ahead. Back in Garland, Mom had endured the agonizing uncertainty of awaiting Dad's return. Their two-year separation magnified her vulnerability, which did not go unnoticed by a former high school sweetheart in Garland, who was now in college and preparing for medical school.

What began as innocent outings—movies, church services, and sundaes at the local pharmacy —rapidly escalated into a brief, intense affair. Overwhelmed by loneliness and a deep longing for connection, Mom sought comfort in a relationship that ultimately led to her unexpected pregnancy. In August 1944, Mom took the Santa Fe Streamliner from Dallas to Los Angeles to spend a few days with Dad in El Centro. The trip was carefully thought out, though hastily arranged, to make it appear as though the conception had occurred during their reunion. However, Dad found the timing of her pregnancy curious, and he noted it in a letter home from El Toro in early 1945: *"Darling, you said in your letter that you thought the baby would come sooner than we had expected..."*

Amid the fog of wartime separations and uncertainties, the questions surrounding Mom's decisions lingered for years. It wasn't until decades later, with the advent of DNA testing, that some clarity began to emerge—though even those findings raised more questions than answers. Years later, while reflecting on those times over lunch with Mimmie, I saw her brow furrow as she fell into deep thought. "I never understood why Betty was so determined to rush across the country to see Howard in the middle of the war," she said, her puzzled expression suggesting she knew more than she was willing to reveal. Her words hung in the air, echoing the unspoken mystery that had cast a shadow over our family for years.

My sister, Carol, was born on March 13, 1945.

Dad never spoke of the war until the day we buried Mom at Dallas' Restland Cemetery in 1996. Returning home from the funeral, he lit an unfiltered Camel and sank into the couch. "You can't imagine how terrified I was as an eighteen-year-old kid, thinking today might be my last day," he said. My Uncle John, who had heard the harrowing details from Dad, once described the sheer terror Dad had felt, strapped into the rear-facing seat of a Helldiver. He painted a vivid picture of the plane plummeting from twelve thousand feet, the sky shrinking above, as a hundred pounds of a .30-caliber Browning machine gun and its ammo belts pressed against Dad's chest. Japanese Zeros screamed down, their gunfire raking the Helldiver. His plane would dive from altitudes between ten thousand and fifteen thousand feet, achieving steep angles for precision bombing, all while Dad braced himself, praying to survive the deadly assault and the treacherous pull-out from the dive.

Then, with a sudden, piercing intensity, he looked in the direction of Carol, who had walked to an adjoining room, pointed a finger, and sneered, *"She's not mine!"* He turned back to me, his eyes burning with a mix of anger and pain, and slowly whispered, "But *you* are!" The air in the room thickened with the weight of his words. The silence that followed was heavy, almost suffocating, before his mood and demeanor took a dark, menacing turn.

"Now, it's time for everybody to leave! Please, get the hell out of here!" His voice was a mix of command and desperation. We hesitated for a moment, unsure and shaken, but the intensity of his gaze propelled us to honor his wishes and leave. The door closed behind us with a finality that echoed through the empty rooms of the house. I never saw Dad again until two years later when we laid him to rest next to Mom in a simple pine box.

His Marine Corps dress uniform, cap, flight jacket, service ribbons, and Purple Heart remained ready for duty in his closet for many years, a silent testament to a life once defined by honor and service. I still have the U.S. flag that draped his coffin, folded meticulously in the triangular military style, a poignant reminder of his life and service to our country and to the battles I never fully understood..

One October day in 2024, an envelope arrived from the U.S. Navy Personnel Command. It had taken nearly five years since I'd first requested them, but there in my hands were my father's World War II commendations: the Air Medal 2, the American Campaign Medal, and his Honorable Discharge. I held them quietly, feeling the weight of what they represented—not just his service in war, but the battles he fought long after the war ended, the ones between him and the world, between him and me.

The Air Medal 2 marked his valor as a Helldiver radio gunner. Every mission he flew, every encounter with the enemy, etched into that medal—each dive could've been his last. These weren't just events recorded in a logbook; they were moments when life hung on a thread.

The American Campaign Medal spoke of his role in a global war, a war fought across oceans and continents, while he faced months of separation, fighting in foreign lands, and enduring hardships I could only begin to imagine.

Then there was the Purple Heart. He earned it when his plane went down near Ulithi. It was more than just recognition of physical wounds—it symbolized the emotional scars that ran deeper than any injury. His Honorable Discharge, simple yet powerful, was the last piece of this puzzle—a final nod to a duty fulfilled, even if the price paid was steep.

For him, those medals must have represented a time when survival, fear, and duty were intertwined, when every day felt like it could be his last. But for me, they stand for something different. They are fragments of a man who, despite his courage, could never fully face the battles within. Our relationship, marked by distance and silence, reflected those unspoken struggles.

Was it the war that pushed him into the grip of alcoholism? The disease that would slowly unravel his life and tear apart our family? It was certainly part of it. But I also wonder if leaving Cleburne—the home of the Burtons for generations—somehow broke him. The sense of dislocation, combined with the horrors he'd seen, surely left him more vulnerable to the stresses of life.

And then there was Mom's infidelity, the betrayal that hovered between them, an unspoken wound that neither seemed able to confront. How he found out, or when, I'll never know. But I'm certain it left its mark. Perhaps that was the final crack, the one that fractured something deep inside him. Maybe it wasn't just one thing, but a slow disintegration—a lifetime of wounds, stacking up one by one.

The medals, the uniform, the folded flag—they tell a story of honor and service, but they can't tell the full story. That part remains locked in silence, somewhere between him and me, in the spaces where love was never spoken, and the battles within were never truly fought.

Carol once told me a story of Mom coming to San Antonio around 1992 to care for her when she had her wisdom teeth extracted. On the second day of her trip, Mom asked to borrow one of their cars for an evening out. Carol was puzzled—her house was in a remote neighborhood, far from any shopping areas or restaurants. Mom took the car and disappeared for hours. When she finally returned late that night, Carol confronted her. "I was seeing an old friend," Mom said. When Carol pressed for more details, Mom replied, "Oh, you wouldn't know them." It turns out her wartime lover had bought a ranch estate in Fair Oaks, Texas, not even a half hour from Carol's home.

Later in life, Mom sought to reconnect with that secret lover, carrying those memories with her for years, waiting for the right moment. But when she finally reached out, he rejected her, telling her he loved his wife and family too much to rekindle anything from the past. Yet, she never fully let go. I found a photograph of him tucked away in a folder she kept hidden—a silent reminder of a chapter in her life she longed to rewrite but never could.

What strikes me most is how, even after being rejected, she spent countless hours caring for this man's mother in her later years. Was it out of love, guilt, or duty? Perhaps, in caring for his mother, she was clinging to the last vestige of that lost connection. This quiet, unseen act of devotion seemed like her way of holding on to a past that had slipped away.

For me, that photograph and the care she gave his mother are symbols of the emotional world she never shared with us—a world of longing and regret, concealed beneath the surface of our everyday lives. As much as she gave to our family, there was always a part of her that remained out of reach, tethered to a love from the past that neither time nor circumstance could erase.

Years later, the questions surrounding our family's past deepened.

Driven by a need for answers, I took a DNA test. Separately, in another time and place, my sister Carol did the same. The results left us with unsettling questions: while my DNA matched both of our parents, Carol's results only fully aligned with Mom's. The differences between our DNA suggested that, while we share the same mother, our paternity was not the same.

And it wasn't just the truth about our paternity that came to light. Amid the revelations about our lineage, an old letter from Gladys Morgan surfaced, shedding new light on Vivian Morgan, the man we had believed was Mom's biological father. In the letter, dated April 1, 1982, Gladys wrote to Mom: "Vivian was an alcoholic. He was always coming and going. He would have temper fits and try to kill us. They had him in the criminally insane ward of the county jail. The doctors and the police told me not to let him come back any more. They told me they would pick him up again if he did. He died in '68—I divorced him in '62."

This revelation about the man I had once believed connected us to a proud heritage only deepened the sense of betrayal I felt. The violent and tragic history, hidden for so long, added another layer of pain to the unraveling of family myths. My DNA also revealed no Native American ancestry, shattering the long-held belief that we had Native American roots through him.

As the illusion of my cherished heritage crumbled, I felt a profound sense of loss and betrayal. The identity I had fiercely claimed, the stories I had woven into my being, were based on a fabrication. Reflecting on these hidden truths, the words of Luke 12:2 came to mind: *"There is nothing concealed that will not be disclosed, or hidden that will not be made known."* The secrets and lies that had long defined our family were finally being revealed, allowing us to confront the past and seek a more honest future.

Amidst this storm of revelations, I often thought of the spiritual rain that seemed to fall upon our family. It was a cleansing force, washing away the dirt of secrets and lies, but also a reminder of the pain that had seeped into the very fabric of our lives. The spiritual rain did not heal everything, but it brought clarity, allowing us to see the truth and, perhaps, to find a path toward peace.

As I grappled with the weight of these revelations, I realized that confronting these hidden truths was the first step toward healing. It was not an easy journey, but one necessary to break the cycle of silence and secrecy. By facing the past with honesty, I could begin to forge a future free from the shadows that had long haunted our family.

CHAPTER 8

Echoes of Violence

The police radio crackled to life, reporting a "10-54," a possible dead body off North Star and Renner roads in far North Garland, and calling for the coroner. I grabbed my camera bag and raced out the door, telling our editor I was tracking a reported fatality out in the sticks. It was 1974, and I was filling in for the regular photographer at *The Garland Daily News* while he vacationed.

The drive took about twenty minutes, and my mind raced with thoughts of what I might find. Arriving at the scene, I saw Garland police cruisers parked silently, their lights flashing a solemn rhythm. I parked and walked over to three officers standing by a ditch, their faces grave as they looked down.

Drawing closer, I saw the lifeless form lying face down in a shallow pool of water, a sight that no amount of preparation could brace me for. One officer noticed me and asked, "Can I help you?"

I pulled out my press pass, saying, "I'm with the newspaper. Here to take some photos."

He took my credentials, giving them a quick glance before handing them back. "Go ahead," he said, "but no close-ups of the body."

With a nod, I moved closer. The male victim lay in a crumpled heap, bullet holes marring his back, neck, and head. He had fallen where he was shot, his final moments ending face down in muddy water tinged with blood. Blood stained his short-sleeved shirt, the scene bearing all the grim trademarks of a gangland slaying. Multiple sets of footprints near the body suggested a struggle had taken place. The moist summer air carried the faint scent of decay and earth, mingling with the distant hum of city life and an occasional passing car.

Violence. I knew it too well. It had shadowed my life for years.

According to statistics, families with a history of alcoholism are significantly more likely to experience violence. Studies reveal that over fifty percent of domestic violence perpetrators have a history of alcohol abuse. This isn't just a statistic; it's a stark illustration of how pervasive and damaging alcoholism can be.

I took several photos, capturing the officers at work, their expressions a mix of routine and resignation. As I drove away, my mind wandered back to a time when violence wasn't just a story to report but a dark reality at home. The blood, the brutality, the stark finality of the crime scene brought back memories of my own childhood.

It was early morning, and after dressing for school, I walked into the den to find Mother sitting in a chair, her face a swollen, bloodied mask. She cradled an ice pack against her bruised eye, tears streaming down her cheeks. I was shocked, almost not recognizing her. "Mom, what happened?" I asked, my voice trembling.

"Last night, I went to the car dealership where your father was working late," she said, her voice weak but steady. "I should have known better. I found him drunk. We fought, and he beat me with a whisky bottle. He tried to strangle me. I thought he was going to kill me...."

The words hung in the air, a dark testament to the violence that had torn through our family. The scene of the crime I had just left felt eerily familiar. The bloodshed, the violence, the unyielding finality of it all – it was a chilling reminder that no matter how far I went, the past was never truly behind me.

As I drove back to the office, the memories mingled with the present, the line between the two blurring. Reporting the news, capturing the grim reality of the world, was my way of coping, of trying to make sense of a life marred by violence. But some days, like today, it felt like the shadows of the past were always just a step behind, waiting to haunt me with where I came from.

In the United States, children growing up in homes with alcohol abuse are four times more likely to experience physical or emotional violence. This reality resonates deeply with me as the echoes of such violence continue to reverberate through my life.

Another Day, Another Echo

On a different day and time, I entered the den before school to find Dad seated with a bloody towel on his face. Mom was nearby, drinking coffee. The room was thick with unspoken tension, the kind that suffocates words before they have a chance to escape.

No one spoke, so I broke the silence: "What's going on here?"

Dad groaned but didn't speak. His eyes were distant, lost in a pain that went beyond the physical.

"Your father was in a car wreck last night," Mom responded, her voice as measured as it was detached. "He was pretty shaken up."

Dad looked as though he had been beaten, his suit jacket ripped, and his tie loosened around his bloodied shirt collar. The sight was a brutal reminder that violence didn't just erupt in loud confrontations; it simmered in the quiet moments, in the aftermath of invisible battles fought within the confines of a twisted mind and broken heart.

Alcohol-related crashes are a significant issue, accounting for nearly thirty percent of all traffic-related deaths in the United States. My father's condition hinted at a darker truth, one that our family knew too well: that alcohol-fueled violence often extends beyond the home, spilling onto the roads and into other facets of life. Thank God he wasn't killed and that no one else had been injured or killed because of his driving under the influence of alcohol.

I knew better than to ask more questions. In our house, answers often came wrapped in layers of silence, delivered in cryptic looks and half-truths. The wreckage of the car seemed almost incidental compared to the wreckage of our lives.

As I left for school, the image of my father, bruised and broken, lingered in my mind.

The presence of violence touched me as a young boy, too. One night, around 11 p.m., I awoke while sleeping on the couch to the sound of my parents in the midst of a terrible argument. Their voices, once muffled, escalated into a crescendo of anger. Suddenly, I heard a thud as Mom struck Dad on the head with the sharp edge of one of my Little League baseball trophies. In retaliation, he grabbed Mom and began hitting her in the head with his fist. That's when I ran and barreled into him with everything I had. The impact sent him sprawling backward into a chair that splintered under his weight. He scrambled to his feet, his eyes burning with rage, and lunged at me, grabbing my pajama top and tossing me around like a rag doll. Terrified, I tore free and ran out the front door, sprinting to the safety of Mimmie's home nearby.

There were no apologies the next morning. In my house, no one ever apologized. Life went on as though nothing had happened.

When I was a teenager, I worked for spending money one summer doing odds and ends at Ray's Garage, an auto repair shop in East Garland. One day, a stocky man in his forties came in to have his car serviced. From the moment he arrived, he began looking at me as though he knew who I was. He waited for the work on his car to be completed, his eyes following me as I moved around the shop.

Finally, he came over and asked, "What's your name?" I told him, and he said, "Is your father Howard Burton?" I nodded yes, and he smiled—a creepy smile that was anything but friendly. "I thought so," he responded sarcastically. "You know, I beat the shit out of your dad one night when I was a policeman." His laugh was sinister, sending a shiver down my spine. He turned around and continued laughing loudly as he walked away.

Reflections and Realities

Back in the present, the sun was beginning to set, casting long shadows across the office parking lot as I returned from the crime scene. The photos I had taken felt heavy in my camera, each frame a testament to the harsh reality of life and death.

Sitting in the darkroom, I reviewed the images, each one a stark reminder of the darkness that lingered just below the surface of everyday life. The faces of the officers, the lifeless form in the ditch, the blood-stained shirt—all were pieces of a puzzle that spoke of a life snuffed out too soon, of violence that left scars not just on the body but on the soul.

As I looked through the photos, I couldn't help but think of my father and the wreckage he had left in his wake. The violence he inflicted wasn't just physical; it was emotional, a slow, corrosive force that ate away at the fabric of our family. And now, decades later, I was still trying to piece together the fragments, to understand the echoes that continued to reverberate through my life.

According to the National Institute on Alcohol Abuse and Alcoholism (NIAAA), children of alcoholics are two to four times more likely to develop problems with alcohol themselves, underscoring the profound impact of alcoholism on family dynamics and individual risk factors. It's a cycle that perpetuates itself, each generation haunted by the shadows of the one before. Violence had shaped me in ways I was only beginning to understand. It had taught me to be cautious, to keep my guard up, to always be ready for the next blow. But it had also given me a strange kind of strength, a resilience forged in the fires of my past. By the grace of God, I've been lucky to enjoy social drinking without falling into the trap of alcoholism that so often affects children of alcoholics.

As I prepared to write the story of the latest tragedy to befall our town, I knew that I was doing more than just reporting the news. I was bearing witness to the echoes of violence that ripple through time, connecting the past to the present, shaping the future in ways that we can't always see but that we can always feel.

Though the past lingered close, it served as a stark reminder of my survival—of facing the darkness and emerging on the other side. In that survival, there was a victory, a defiance that declared, *"I'm still here. I'm still standing. I'm still fighting."*

As the last light of day faded and the office grew quiet, I began to type, each word a small act of resistance against the violence that had tried to define me, each sentence a step toward reclaiming the story of my life from the shadows of the past.

CHAPTER 9

The Silence of the Stones

In the years since I began untangling the web of my childhood, one question has lingered like an unwelcome shadow: Why didn't anyone intervene? Why did my grandparents, aunts, uncles, and other relatives watch from the sidelines while the conflict between Mom and Dad unfolded before us? The absence of intervention from the adults in our lives seemed, at times, as painful as the dysfunction itself. Were they complicit? Why did they choose silence over action?

The story of the hunger stones in Central Europe has always resonated with me. These stones, visible only when water levels are dangerously low, bear inscriptions from the past—warnings of famine and hardship. They emerge when the river's flow is at its weakest, much like the truths that surface during the most challenging times in our lives. Growing up, our home was like a river running dry, revealing hidden stones etched with silent suffering. The emotional drought brought forth the hunger stones of our existence—moments of crisis that exposed the deep-rooted conflict between my parents. These stones marked the times when their battles spilled over, leaving scars on us children that were visible only to those who dared to look closely.

As children, we learned the unspoken rules: don't talk about it, don't trust anyone with it, and don't feel anything about it. These were the inscriptions on our personal hunger stones, lessons learned from living in the shadow of dysfunction. Much like the warnings on those ancient stones, these rules were passed down silently, shaping our perceptions and responses to the world around us.

One of the few adults who would ask me about home was my grandmother, Mimmie, who brought me to Christ and who gave me my first real Bible on my birthday in 1977. She inscribed it: *"Please make this Bible your daily companion. Love, ever, Mimmie."* She'd invite me to have lunch or dessert in her kitchen, a sanctuary from the chaos. Her voice was soft, always a little hesitant, as if she wasn't sure she should ask but felt compelled to try.

"What's happening at home, Keith?" she'd ask, her eyes full of concern.

If I mentioned anything that hinted at the turmoil between Mom and Dad, she would pause, her face tightening ever so slightly, and reply with a simple, "Oh?" It was a small word, a placeholder for all the things left unsaid, carrying a weight of understanding and helplessness.

Mimmie's "Oh" was more than just a word. It was an acknowledgment of what she perhaps couldn't bring herself to fully confront or discuss. It was the quiet recognition that things were not right, even if she couldn't or wouldn't say more. Her response often left me feeling both seen and abandoned, a bittersweet mix of understanding and isolation.

In contrast, Granddaddy and Grandmother Burton never asked about our home life. Their greeting was always the same: cookies, cakes, and pies spread out like a feast, accompanied by laughter that felt hollow. Their joviality seemed an attempt to fill the void of unspoken truths, a sugary distraction from the darkness that loomed over our family.

The sweets were meant to comfort, but they only highlighted what was missing—a genuine inquiry into our lives, a willingness to see beyond the facade. Their laughter, although warm, felt empty because it never bridged the gap to our reality. It was as if they were trying to create a bubble of happiness where no pain could enter, a temporary escape from the reality they chose not to see.

I've come to understand that cultural and generational factors played a significant role in the silence of my extended family. My grandparents and their peers were raised in a time when family issues were considered private matters. The concept of airing one's dirty laundry was anathema, a betrayal of familial loyalty. They believed in handling problems internally, a notion rooted in pride and perhaps a misplaced sense of duty. Admitting there was a problem with alcohol and conflict would have shattered the facade of normalcy they were desperate to maintain.

The silence wasn't new. Great Uncle "Unk" Howard Jennings returned from World War I a changed man. During the war, he was exposed to mustard gas, a chemical weapon known for its mustard color and garlic-like odor. While the immediate mortality rate was low, the gas caused severe chemical burns and respiratory issues. Victims often endured long hospital stays, and many suffered long-term health problems, including an increased risk of cancer. The physical and psychological scars haunted Unk, leading him to drown his trauma in alcohol. His first wife endured his descent in silence for years, her suffering tucked away behind closed doors until she finally found the courage to leave, divorcing him in a time when such an act was nearly unthinkable.

Despite her brave decision, there seemed to be no way out for those of us left behind. The stigma attached to alcoholism and family dysfunction in those days was a heavy burden. Relatives might have feared that acknowledging the problem would bring shame upon the family name. It was easier, safer, to turn a blind eye than to confront the ugly truth and risk becoming social pariahs. Perhaps they believed that by ignoring the problem, it might somehow resolve itself or, at the very least, remain hidden from public scrutiny.

Denial is a powerful, often insidious force. It can twist reality, making the intolerable seem tolerable and the unacceptable acceptable. For my relatives, confronting the truth meant facing their own fears and limitations. It meant stepping into a role they felt ill-equipped to handle. The idea of intervening might have seemed overwhelming, the potential fallout too great to bear. And so, they chose avoidance, pretending not to see the emotional drought that was leaving its mark on us children.

Fear can paralyze even the most well-intentioned individuals. My relatives might have feared the repercussions of intervening, worried that they would only exacerbate the situation or become alienated from my parents. Perhaps they felt trapped between loyalty to their own children and the well-being of their grandchildren. This fear, compounded by a lack of understanding of alcoholism's true nature, kept them in the shadows, reluctant to step into the light.

As I've grown older, I've learned to recognize that everyone carries their own burdens. Some of my relatives had their own struggles—health issues, financial difficulties, or other dysfunctional family dynamics—that consumed their attention and resources. It's possible they simply didn't have the emotional or physical capacity to extend help, even if they wanted to.

There's a painful truth in acknowledging that some relatives might have enabled my parents' behavior, not out of malice, but out of misguided loyalty or love. By providing financial support or making excuses, they may have inadvertently allowed the dysfunction to continue unchecked. It's a difficult realization, knowing that what was intended as support only served to reinforce the cycle of addiction and conflict.

Reflecting on these possibilities doesn't erase the pain of those years, but it helps me make sense of the silence that surrounded us. It's a complex tapestry of fear, denial, stigma, and misguided loyalty that wove the fabric of my childhood. Understanding this complexity is a step toward healing, a way to lay to rest the hunger stones that have long marked the droughts of my past.

In this journey of recovery and healing, I'm reminded of Matthew 5:14-16: *"You are the light of the world. A town built on a hill cannot be hidden. Neither do people light a lamp and put it under a bowl. Instead, they put it on its stand, and it gives light to everyone in the house. In the same way, let your light shine before others, that they may see your good deeds and glorify your Father in heaven."* These verses serve as a guiding principle, encouraging me to break the silence that was once my inheritance and let the truth shine.

I'm committed to breaking the cycle for future generations, ensuring that they grow up in a world where silence doesn't mean complicity and where intervention isn't a question but a given. It's a legacy of awareness and action, one that honors the truth rather than hiding from it, transforming those silent stones into stepping stones toward a healthier future.

CHAPTER 10

Shadows of Panic

In the years following my escape from the violence and dysfunction of home, I thought I had left the worst behind me. After graduating from high school, college was supposed to be my fresh start, a chance to reinvent myself away from the shadows of my past. But it wasn't long before those shadows caught up with me in an unexpected and terrifying way.

I remember the first time it happened, at age eighteen. For months, I had been working twelve-hour shifts at the newspaper while attending college. I barely got any sleep, surviving on just two to four hours a night. I smoked two packs of cigarettes a day and drank copious amounts of coffee to stay awake. On top of that, my diet was poor. The relentless grind was unsustainable, and my body finally rebelled.

One morning, as I was typing a news story at my desk, my heart suddenly began to race. My chest tightened as if a vise had clamped around it, and my breaths came in shallow, rapid gasps. My vision blurred, and a cold sweat broke out across my forehead. I felt a surge of pure, unadulterated terror.

"Am I dying?" I whispered to myself, unable to think straight or focus on anything but the overwhelming fear that had gripped me. I bolted

from the office, my legs unsteady, and stumbled outside into the fresh air, hoping it would help. It didn't. The panic continued to swell inside me, a relentless wave crashing over me again and again.

I returned to the office to gather my things and then got into the car to drive home. Another wave hit me unbidden. I remember gripping the steering wheel so tightly my knuckles turned white. *"Just breathe!"* I told myself, but my breaths were short and frantic, the walls of the car closing in around me.

The traffic lights blurred, the sounds of honking horns and the rush of passing cars fading into a distant hum. I struggled to keep my eyes on the road, but my vision tunneled, the edges growing darker with each passing second. Sweat trickled down my temples, and I fought the urge to pull over and abandon the car right there on the side of Garland Road.

Every instinct screamed at me to escape, but where could I go? I was trapped, a prisoner to my own panic. *"I'm alone,"* I muttered, the realization intensifying the fear. My mind raced through worst-case scenarios: losing control of the car, crashing, dying.

I fumbled for the window handle, lowering it in a futile attempt to gulp in the morning air. The breeze did little to calm my racing heart or ease the tightness in my chest.

Minutes felt like hours as I navigated the streets, each turn of the wheel a monumental effort. Somehow, I made it home, the familiar sight of our house a small comfort in the chaos. I parked, turned off the engine, and sat there, trembling, unable to move.

Tears streamed down my face as I struggled to regain control, the realization dawning that this was something far beyond my understanding or control. This was my new reality, a hidden, insidious monster that could strike without warning.

When I went inside and told Mom what had happened, she immediately picked up the phone and called the doctor's office to schedule an appointment. That day marked the beginning of a fifty-year journey through a labyrinth of anxiety. I sought help, starting with visits to doctors and therapists. They explained that what I was experiencing was a manifestation of the anxiety and trauma that had been simmering beneath the surface for years.

Research has shown that children of alcoholics are particularly susceptible to anxiety disorders, including panic attacks. Studies indicate that we're more likely to experience higher levels of anxiety and panic disorders compared to those from non-alcoholic families. This increased vulnerability is often attributed to the chronic stress and trauma experienced during childhood, which can disrupt normal emotional development and coping mechanisms.

During one of my earliest appointments, I asked our family physician, "How long will it take to get over these panic attacks?"

He looked at me thoughtfully. "How long did it take before you had your first panic attack?" he asked rhetorically. "We don't know. By the same token, it will take time and understanding to fully recover."

I was prescribed medication, which offered some relief but came with its own set of challenges. Side effects, adjustments, and the constant fear of dependency were my new companions. Counseling sessions became a regular part of my life, each one attempting to peel back layers of fear and pain, revealing the deeply rooted scars left by years of dysfunction and alcoholism at home.

In the beginning, living with anxiety was a daily battle. It struck without warning, often triggered by stress, crowded places, or even just the anticipation of an attack. Each episode was a reminder of the fragility of my peace and the tenuous grip I had on normalcy. I endured these panic attacks through every seminal period in my life—college, marriage, raising a family, during two major health challenges my wife faced, and working in some of the most challenging news reporting and leadership roles in the fields of journalism and public relations.

One particularly vivid memory from my childhood came back to me during these times. While driving in our neighborhood one morning, I recall Mom veering off the street, crashing our car into a neighbor's yard, and destroying their shrubbery and a picket fence. It was scary. She later told me it was because of a panic attack. This revelation deepened my understanding of the hereditary nature of anxiety and the shared struggles within our family.

"Why didn't you tell me?" I asked her one evening, desperate to understand.

"I didn't want to worry you," she said softly. "I thought it was my burden to bear alone."

Her experience became a source of empathy and connection, knowing that she, too, had fought similar battles in silence.

Over the years, I learned various coping mechanisms to manage my anxiety. Deep breathing exercises, mindfulness techniques, and grounding exercises became my lifelines. Dr. Claire Weekes, a general practitioner and health writer who pioneered modern anxiety treatment, was an early beacon of hope with her books and tapes on dealing with anxiety disorders.

Later, I was fortunate to find psychologists in Dallas and Naperville, Illinois, who specialized in treating OCD, phobias, and PTSD. These psychologists were more than just professionals; they were guides on my journey to self-discovery. They helped me unlock the secrets of my childhood, unraveling the deep-seated traumas that fueled my anxiety. Through their guidance, I learned to reframe my thoughts, confront my past, and develop effective strategies to manage my anxiety. Their support was invaluable, transforming my understanding of mental health and paving the way for my recovery.

While I relied on coping mechanisms and medication for years, it wasn't until I truly confronted my past that I could fully overcome the anxiety. Facing the buried pain, acknowledging the traumas, and understanding their impact allowed me to reclaim my true self and heal my lost inner child.

Reflecting on those years, I see a journey marked by perseverance and struggle. Each anxious episode was a battle fought and survived, a testament to my will to overcome the shadows of my past. Through it all, I discovered a strength I never knew I had—a relentless determination to reclaim my life from fear. True healing comes from within, and my journey is a testament to the power of facing one's demons and emerging stronger.

CHAPTER 11

The Thesis That Saved Me

Our greatest fear in life should not be failure,
but in succeeding in things that don't really matter."
—Francis Chan, American Protestant author, teacher, and preacher

When I was a boy, death was not an enemy. Its presence brought peace and new beginnings—feelings I still connect with decades after my Pawpaw's death at age sixty-seven from a heart attack. He was buried on a cold November day in 1962. The bitter wind, the crimson sky, and the preacher's comforting words at the open grave are vivid memories that stay with me.

On April 19, 1980, I found myself reflecting on life and death as I drove south toward the Texas Gulf Coast. Five months earlier, in a bioethics course taught by Dr. Richard Zaner at Southern Methodist University in Dallas, I had watched a videotape about Donald Cowart, a man severely burned in a 1973 propane explosion. The tape, *Please Let Me Die*, documented Cowart's plea to refuse medical treatment and end his life. As a working journalist, my curiosity about his fate led me to Galveston, where I would meet him for the first time.

The story of Don Cowart, or "Dax," as he later became known, is both extraordinary and commonplace. Raised in East Texas, he was an athlete, a pilot in Vietnam, and a man with a promising future. But his life changed forever on July 23, 1973, when a propane explosion left him with severe burns over sixty-five percent of his body. His father died, and Don's subsequent treatment was excruciating.

Ray, a real estate agent, and his son, Don, had driven out to a ranch to inspect some property. After surveying the land, they returned to their car, which was parked on a bridge over a dry creek bed. When the car wouldn't start, Ray primed the carburetor, causing a blue flame to ignite a propane gas pocket from a leaking pipeline. The gas was odorless, and so the men wouldn't have detected it. The resulting explosion hurled Ray into the underbrush and engulfed Don in flames. Despite his severe burns, Don managed to run through walls of fire to seek help for his father. A farmer found him gravely injured and refused Don's desperate plea for a gun that he would use to end his life.

Don was taken to Parkland Hospital in Dallas, where he began a 232-day ordeal of treatments that included debridement, skin grafts, and amputations. His face and hands were severely disfigured, and he lost his right eye. Throughout this time, Don persistently asked to be allowed to die, but his pleas were dismissed by his medical team, led by Dr. Charles Baxter, and his family, particularly his mother, Ada. It was later determined that Don would be blind in both eyes, adding to the severity of his injuries and his desire to end his suffering.

Ada was tormented by her son's suffering but could not condone ending his life. Her religious beliefs and fear that Don had not made peace with God reinforced her resolve to support his treatment. Similarly, their attorney, Rex Houston, needed Don alive to secure a favorable legal settlement for his injuries, ensuring financial stability for Don's future care.

In February 1974, Don's lawsuit against the pipeline company was settled, and his demands to die intensified. He asked friends and medical staff to help him end his life, but all refused. Don was then transferred to the Texas Institute for Research and Rehabilitation (TIRR) in Houston, where he was given more control over his treatment decisions. However, the realization that his pain might be permanent led him to refuse further treatment and nourishment, nearly resulting in his death.

At TIRR, Don's condition worsened, leading to his transfer to the burn unit at John Sealy Hospital at the University of Texas Medical Branch (UTMB) in Galveston. There, Dr. Duane Larson and psychiatrist Dr. Robert White evaluated him, determining that Don was mentally competent despite his persistent desire to die. Dr. White recorded an interview with Don, titled *Please Let Me Die*, which became a significant case study in patient rights and medical ethics.

Despite his continued resistance to treatment, Don's condition gradually improved under Dr. White's care. He was weaned off heavy sleep medications, which alleviated his depression. By July 1974, Don consented to necessary surgeries, and by September he was discharged to continue his recovery at home.

Back in Henderson, Texas, Don's struggle continued. He faced daily pain, disfigurement, and complete dependence on others. Depression led to multiple suicide attempts. With encouragement from Rex Houston, Don tried pursuing a law degree at Baylor University School of Law. Despite his determination, the challenges were immense, and he dropped out twice before finally completing his law degree at Texas Tech University in 1986.

Don's resilience shone through as he rebuilt his life. He started a mail-order business, which later failed; became a vocal advocate for patient rights; and passed the bar exam. His journey, documented in *Dax's Case*, the 1984 documentary film I co-produced with Don Pasquella, a film professor in the Meadows School of the Arts at SMU, showcased his transformation from a man seeking death to one fighting for the right to make his own choices.

With the aid of assistive devices, Don established his own law practice and later worked with trial attorney Robert Hilliard, founder of Hilliard Munoz Gonzales LLC in Corpus Christi, Texas. He legally changed his first name to "Dax" in the summer of 1982 to avoid confusion, given his blindness and difficulty in hearing, and because the shorter name was easier for him to write.

Dax married Samantha Berryessa, a California attorney, and they lived on a farm in San Diego County. He was previously married to Sharla L. Stone in 1971 and Karen Bolton in 1983, both of which ended in divorce.

Dax was a frequent teacher and speaker at the Trial Lawyers College in Dubois, Wyoming, founded by Gerry Spence. Motivated by his personal experience and professional background, Dax became a prominent patient rights advocate. He continuously argued for patient autonomy and the right to choose, even if that choice meant death. His experience became a famous bioethics case, illustrating several issues of patient autonomy.

Dax's life and reflections challenged medicine's understanding of itself as a moral practice. He spoke on patient rights in the US and abroad. In addition to *Dax's Case*, his journey was documented in multiple films, including *Please Let Me Die*, an ABC News 20/20 segment titled "Dax's Story" (1999), and *Dax Cowart: 40 Years Later* (2013). He was also interviewed by major newspapers, magazines, and medical publications through the years.

Dax Cowart died at the age of seventy-one on April 28, 2019, from complications of leukemia and liver cancer in Fallbrook, California.

Looking back on my life and work, the making of *Dax's Case* stands out as my greatest career achievement. As a student in a medical ethics class, I was driven to find a man whose vibrant life was shattered by a tragic accident and to bring his story to life. In moments of dark despair, he plotted ways to end his life—jumping from a hospital window, attempting to slash his badly scarred wrists, overdosing on pain medication, or throwing himself in front of a fast-moving pulpwood truck near his rural home in East Texas. Instead, Don ultimately found purpose in telling his story and passionately advocating for patient autonomy and the right to choose.

For me, this became a very personal story. In early 1980, Don came for a weekend stay at our home in Garland. Those forty-eight hours were intensely moving. I experienced firsthand the gravity of his injuries and the extent of his helplessness in carrying out daily tasks like eating, performing bodily functions, bathing, and dressing himself. Witnessing his struggle, I felt a deep sadness, yet also an overwhelming love for a fellow human being enduring such immense suffering. His resilience and determination to advocate for patient rights despite his pain left an indelible mark on me.

Making *Dax's Case* was both cathartic and illuminating. We created a company to produce and distribute the film. Working with Concern for Dying, a New York not-for-profit, the Texas Committee for the Humanities, and private donors, we raised more than half a million dollars to produce it. I conducted extensive research, interviewed Don and the film's cast members many times, and collaborated with scholars, bioethicists, and medical and legal professionals to accurately portray his story. When it finally premiered in the Bob Hope Theater at SMU in 1985, I still remember the exhilaration I felt for bringing this life-altering project to fruition.

The five-year project culminated in a comprehensive documentary film that not only served as my thesis but also gained significant recognition by winning prestigious awards at the American Film Festival and the John Muir Medical Film Festival. The accolades were a testament to the film's impact and the importance of Dax's story.

Perhaps the highest recognition, however, came from the Weill Cornell Medicine School at Cornell University. For many years, they've used *Dax's Case* as a teaching tool for nursing and allied health students. A faculty member once remarked that he considered *Dax's Case* the most powerful storytelling tool available for illustrating a patient's autonomy and the right to choose.

It's not lost on me that after I first met Dax in 1980, the man who wanted to die embarked on a life of remarkable productivity and profound influence for the next thirty-nine years. His journey became a catalyst for deep and transformative discussions at universities and medical schools and among caregivers.

Dax didn't just advocate for the right to make personal choices about health care treatment; he revolutionized the conversation around patient autonomy and the right to die. His unwavering dedication and powerful voice inspired countless individuals, fundamentally changing the way we perceive medical ethics and human dignity. Through his relentless advocacy, Dax left an indelible mark on the world, challenging us to rethink our deepest beliefs about life, death, and the essence of human rights.

The making of *Dax's Case* and its subsequent recognition was a pivotal step in my emergence from the shadows of my past. It transformed my pain into purpose, as I advocated for patient rights and helped others navigate their struggles. Reflecting on those years, I see a journey marked by perseverance. Each anxious episode, much like Dax's battles, was a testament to our will to overcome the past. I overcame the damaging impact of my father's alcoholism and the destructive choices made by those around me, emerging stronger and more resolute in my quest for healing and self-discovery.

In the end, Dax taught me that our greatest achievement is not in succeeding at things that don't matter, but in fighting for the things that truly do. His story, and my small part in it, redefined my understanding of success and purpose. It's a lesson that continues to guide me, reminding me of the profound impact one life can have on another.

CHAPTER 12

Revolving Around the Sun

The sleek, bustling lobby of the Pan Am Building greeted me as the elevator doors slid open. It was the mid-'80s, and I was here for a pivotal breakfast meeting that could steer my career onto a new path. As I stepped into this grand space, my nerves buzzed with anticipation. The gravity of the occasion wasn't lost on me. I had worked tirelessly for Hill & Knowlton, Inc., the prestigious New York-headquartered PR agency, and now, my efforts might culminate in becoming the general manager of the Dallas office.

That morning, Robert L. Dilenschneider, the firm's president and CEO, had flown in by helicopter from JFK Airport. As I awaited his arrival in the executive dining room, the polished professionalism around me starkly contrasted with the turbulent chaos of my early life. I found myself reflecting on those difficult years, my thoughts weaving between past and present, connecting the emotional dots that led me here.

My mother's emotional and mental turmoil had cast long shadows over my childhood in the '60s and '70s. Her increasing co-dependency in the wake of my father's alcoholism forced us, her children, to become unwilling anchors in her storm. As she grew more controlling, the boundary between her needs and ours blurred. We were extensions of her, each tasked with holding her together even as we navigated our own turbulent waters.

Echoing in my mind were the words from Psalm 102: *"My days are like the evening shadow; I wither away like grass."* Those years did indeed feel like a slow withering, each day a struggle against the encroaching darkness. Yet, here I was, in a place of potential and promise, seeking a future that seemed so distant during those troubled times.

An imposing figure, Dilenschneider stormed into the room from the rooftop helipad, the sound of Sikorsky helicopter rotors still echoing above us. He greeted me with a vise-like handshake, his steely, intense demeanor setting the tone. We sat for breakfast, and he wasted no time. "What makes you think you should be the GM of the Dallas office?" he probed, his penetrating gaze challenging me.

Gathering my thoughts, I told him why I believed I was qualified, outlining my achievements and vision for the office. He took it in, his expression unreadable. Then, he slowly shook his head, a subtle but definitive gesture, as if dismissing an errant notion. "You're not ready yet," he said. The words struck me like buckshot from a shotgun blast to the face.

The waiter's arrival with our breakfast interrupted us, bringing a momentary reprieve from the tension. "Here, let's eat," Dilenschneider commanded. I mechanically picked at my scrambled eggs, my appetite lost to nerves. The room fell silent except for the soft clinks of silverware and rustle of cloth napkins.

After a long, awkward pause, Dilenschneider softened. "I'm sorry about this morning. You know, I have what they call 'King's Disease,' and I'm sometimes not in the best of moods. My apologies if I've been too direct."

King's Disease, better known as gout, was a painful form of arthritis that often afflicted those with rich diets who overindulged, historically associated with royalty and the wealthy. This admission, a rare glimpse into his personal struggles, reminded me of the immense pressures and expectations tied to such high status.

We exchanged a few more pleasantries about college sports, his Notre Dame Fighting Irish, and his newest client before he excused himself. "My car is ready downstairs, and I have a meeting across town. Can I drop you anywhere?" I declined and thanked him for his time.

As he left, I sat there, feeling a wash of inadequacy—a familiar ache rooted deeply in the turmoil of my upbringing. Despite my professional accomplishments, these moments brought me back to the helplessness of my childhood, supporting my mother amid her spiraling illness. The echoes of those years reverberated through my mind, amplifying my sense of defeat.

Imagine being twelve years old, clad in your pajamas, the comfort of your bed abruptly traded for the cold back seat of a station wagon. My mother, with hurried hands and a set jaw, pulled my infant sister and brother from their beds, wrapping them tightly against the autumn chill. The crisp air bit at my face as we piled into the car, the night draped in a heavy blanket of urgency.

"Mom, why are we doing this?" I asked. Her silence hung thick before she finally spoke, a forced cheer in her voice. "You'll see. We're going on a little adventure!" It was 9:15 p.m.—the dashboard clock glowing softly in the dark, a silent witness to the long night ahead, promising little sleep before school. In his car seat, Kurtis's soft whimpers melded with the steady hum of the engine, a lullaby none of us could heed.

We traveled from Skillman to Northwest Highway, turning off into Vickery Park's more decrepit quarters. The neighborhood wore its neglect like a cloak: dimly lit homes with windows casting ghostly reflections on cracked sidewalks, the relics of junked cars, and untamed lawns. Flickering streetlights cast dancing shadows, crafting an eerie tableau as our wagon crept through the dark streets.

Mom slowed to a halt, scrutinizing a mailbox before turning sharply into a driveway. The beams of our headlights bathed the house in stark light as she parked and sprinted to the front porch. The screen door creaked and squeaked as it swung open, letting out a gentle whoosh before a soft thud as it settled against the frame. Then, with a sense of purpose, Mom knocked three times. The sound sliced through the quiet night like a verdict.

From the car, we watched, breaths caught in anxious holds, as the front door eventually creaked open to reveal a shadowy figure. Their conversation, a murmured exchange of urgent whispers, ended with a nod before the figure retreated and shut the door.

Mom trudged back to our car, got in, and slammed the door shut. She shifted into reverse, the tires squealing on the asphalt as we lurched backward into the street before shifting forward and speeding off. Silence filled the car as she navigated back onto Skillman, her hands tightly gripping the steering wheel. Eventually, she began to cry. "Your dad was in there with his whore!" she wailed. "That's all I wanted to know." The night's chaotic journey had confirmed her worst fears, but it had come at the cost of our time and emotional energy. We drove home in silence, the weight of the evening settling heavily upon us, the destination and the heartbreak feeling equally inevitable.

This wasn't the first time our family had been drawn into such a fruitless pursuit. On another occasion, we found ourselves embroiled in a similar ordeal in the quaint town of Winnsboro, Texas. Despite its picturesque charm and the festive backdrop of the annual Autumn Leaves Festival, Winnsboro became the unlikely stage for a painful family confrontation.

We had paused at a mini market near Lake Tawakoni to gather snacks and beverages, a brief respite before continuing our autumnal journey to witness the season's changing leaves. The flickering neon lights of the market cast an unsettling glow over the parking lot, fore-shadowing the discomfort ahead. As we emerged from the store, the pit of my stomach dropped at the sight unfolding before us. My father, noticeably inebriated, was staggering toward the entrance, a mysterious red-haired woman clinging to his side, their raucous laughter piercing the brisk air. My voice trembled as I called out to Mom. She turned, her gasp cutting through the chill, her eyes wide with shock.

"Howard, how could you!" she cried out. My father, his gaze blurry and unfocused, offered no words, simply continuing into the store with his companion. "You spend your weekends with this witch while leaving your real family behind!" Mom screamed, her voice echoing in the lot, drawing the stares of passersby. Flushed with humiliation, we hurried back to the car, and Mom drove us home at a feverish pace.

From my earliest memories, Mom had been a constant presence at bedtime, her nightly visits a comforting ritual. She would pray with me, sing "Jesus Loves Me" or "Now I Lay Me Down to Sleep," and share tales of Little Betty, or ask me about my day's activities. This routine, once a source of security, gradually felt more like a tether as I entered adolescence, the comfort replaced by a suffocating closeness.

The first time I was touched by death was when Unk's wonderful wife, Paula, suffered a brain aneurysm and died in her sleep. When I found out about her passing at age five, I went into the backyard and hid by the slide. I remember crying, the weight of loss settling heavily on my young heart.

When Aunt Paula died, Mom didn't let me go to the funeral, fearing it would be too traumatic. Instead, I was left wondering why I couldn't say goodbye to my beloved aunt. This confusion and pain lingered, creating a deep sense of longing and unresolved grief. I wanted to honor her memory, but I was denied that closure. Over the years, this early encounter with death, and the feelings of exclusion and helplessness it brought, added layers to my anxiety. It was a profound lesson in the importance of farewells and the emotional turmoil that comes with the inability to find closure.

When it was time for me to start first grade, Mom decided to hold me back a year. Confused and disappointed, I watched as my friends advanced without me, leaving me behind to grapple with a sense of inadequacy and bewilderment. The decision felt like a judgment on my capabilities, a silent accusation that I wasn't ready to keep pace with my peers. When I later confronted her about it, she offered an explanation that felt flimsy and unconvincing: She believed that my being left-handed and, in her eyes, too young, justified the delay. This rationale never quite settled with me, leaving an enduring question mark over that pivotal moment in my young life.

Her reluctance to let me grow independent was palpable. It was less about my readiness for life's challenges and more about her compulsion to keep me under her watchful eye. This overbearing need for control permeated her decisions, reflecting not just a desire for order but a profound struggle to let go, each choice echoing her deep-seated fears and insecurities.

In the universe of our family, Mom was the sun, and we, her children, the planets in orbit. Her presence exerted a gravitational pull that dictated the trajectories of our lives. Each decision and each action we undertook was influenced by her needs and desires. My siblings and I learned to navigate her emotional climate—dodging the storms of her mood swings and basking in the rare warmth of her approval. We revolved around her, each of us playing our roles in maintaining the fragile equilibrium of our family cosmos.

As I matured, her need for control intensified. She would go to great lengths to govern my life, citing the dangers of alcohol and romantic relationships as if they were life-threatening perils. "Alcohol will ruin your life," she would warn, her stories of addiction and downfall laden with emotional intensity. She painted my father's battles with alcoholism as dire warnings, her voice fraught with fear and resolve.

Dating became a minefield. She scrutinized my interactions with girls, convinced that any romantic involvement was a recipe for disaster. "They'll distract you from your goals," she insisted, setting strict curfews and grilling me about my companions and whereabouts. Her control reached its peak one afternoon when, in a fit of rage over my planned meet-up with a girlfriend at a basketball game, she hurled a plate at my feet. It shattered, slicing deep into my left ankle and leaving a bloody mess that sidelined me for the weekend.

It always struck me as particularly controlling and hypocritical that Mom insisted we attend Sunday School, church services, and Vacation Bible School during the summer, yet she never made any effort to join us.

She would ensure we were properly dressed and fed before dropping us off and picking us up later. Similarly, she made sure I was always sent off to baseball, basketball, track, and football practices, yet she and Dad never attended any of my games or meets. It was more than disheartening; it felt as if they were merely ticking off boxes, fulfilling obligations without genuine involvement. I was present, doing as expected and desired on my part, but the absence of those who should have been my biggest supporters left a more profound imprint than any religious sermon or athletic triumph ever could. Their neglect marked me deeper than the cheers of any crowd, echoing the silence of empty bleachers at every game.

Her need to control infiltrated every aspect of my life, from my friendships to my academic endeavors. She would scrutinize my schoolwork, often sitting beside me for hours to ensure each assignment met her exacting standards. She aimed for me to achieve straight As, a goal I consistently met. What might have been perceived as supportive guidance felt more akin to surveillance, a perpetual reminder of her dominance over my choices.

The emotional burden of her oppressive presence was overwhelming. I often felt ensnared, struggling to carve out my own identity while being incessantly drawn back by her pervasive fears and anxieties. Her cautions, though intended as protective measures, morphed into shackles that constrained and suffocated me beneath the heavy mantle of her expectations.

These experiences profoundly shaped my conception of freedom and control. I became adept at navigating her moods, seizing small opportunities for autonomy whenever possible, yet the shadow of her influence loomed large. It took years to extricate myself from her clutches fully, to realize that her controlling nature stemmed from her deep-seated insecurities and fears, and to chart my own course forward.

Life is a series of choices, as Mom often reminded me. Each decision, no matter how insignificant it might seem, shapes the trajectory of our lives. I learned this the hard way, growing up with an alcoholic parent and enduring the lasting impact on our family dynamics. My mother's life was also defined by her choices, from revelations about her heritage to the agonizing decisions she faced during her panic attacks and her extramarital affair while Dad was away at war. Each choice carried the weight of countless consequences.

Mom chose to conceal the truth about her adoption, profoundly affecting our understanding of identity and heritage. Later, DNA testing shattered the illusion of our Native American ancestry, revealing the complex web of decisions that shaped our family's history. Her affair not only fractured their marriage but cast a long shadow over our family, altering trust, loyalty, and love. The ripple effects of her actions added complexity to our relationships, fundamentally shaping who I became.

Reflecting now, I see how each decision, secret, and revelation intricately molded our lives. Life is not merely about significant events but also about the choices made in quiet, unguarded moments.

These decisions have left impressions deeper than any triumph or setback could.

In college, when panic attacks began to overwhelm me, I was faced with a critical decision: seek help or let the fear overpower me. For decades, I chose medication and counseling, a route my mother had navigated for decades. Her battles with anxiety mirrored my own, highlighting the hereditary nature of our struggles.

My involvement with Dax Cowart was another defining moment of choice. Witnessing his fight for the right to die confronted me with the profound ethical and personal dilemmas that shape our humanity. His story, much like my own, underscored the impact of choice and the inevitable consequences that follow.

These experiences have led me to understand how each choice has steered me to where I am today. My decision to address the dysfunction within our family, to share my story, and to combat the stigma and shame associated with it all derive from a desire to illuminate the darkness. This journey has been a sequence of difficult farewells and treasured greetings, each marking a pivotal change in my path.

Ultimately, karma never forgets an address. The choices we make resonate through our lives and those of others. By acting with integrity and compassion, we aspire to leave a legacy of positive change. My memoir stands as a testament to the choices made, the challenges faced, and the relentless pursuit of truth and healing.

Years later, when I took the helm as GM at the Ketchum office in Chicago, I found an envelope on my desk with familiar handwriting—a note from Bob Dilenschneider. Despite having long departed H&K and leading his own firm, Bob's congratulations and good wishes were a constant in my career. From overseeing the Chicago office and Midwest region at H&K to leading operations at Golin Harris in Chicago and Dallas, and as president of Insidedge, Bob's notes always arrived on my first day.

These messages were more than courtesies; they were powerful reminders that amidst the relentless demands of leadership, grace and kindness leave the deepest impressions. This enduring legacy of mentorship and goodwill shaped my career, teaching me the profound impact of our interactions on others. Reflecting on my journey, I realize that true leadership lies in the grace and kindness we extend to those we lead, creating a lasting legacy of positive influence.

CHAPTER 13

It's the Journey, Not the Destination

It was Day Four of our six-day climb of Mount Kilimanjaro in Tanzania. We rose early again, greeted by the biting cold of the morning sunshine and temperatures that felt like they could freeze the soul. Given a precious bowl of hot water to wash up, we quickly freshened up and enjoyed a hearty breakfast at the Horombo Huts.

On my flight to Kili from Nairobi, Kenya, a few days earlier at an altitude of 17,000 feet, I was struck by the fact that this magnificent mountain is so tall that it makes its own weather. Today promised to be particularly grueling, with the sky clear and Kili's imposing peak visible in all its glory. We set off, knowing we had a six- to eight-hour hike ahead of us, crossing the eerie lunar desert of the Saddle between Mawenzi Peak and the Kibo Huts. Over the six miles we would cover, the elevation would climb from 12,205 feet to a breath-stealing 15,430 feet. The peak and its glaciers loomed ever larger, a constant, daunting reminder of both the progress we'd made and the formidable challenge still ahead to reach the summit.

It was January 2006, and I was fifty-one years old. As we began our trip at the Kili airport a few days earlier, my good friend and the organizer of our summit expedition, Dr. Peter Hammerschmidt, a professor of economics at Eckerd College and a renowned authority on leadership development, gathered our group of twenty-four students and business leaders to discuss what lay ahead.

"We're on an adventure," Peter told the group. "Webster's definition of 'adventure' is an exciting event that contains elements of risk or danger and where the outcome is uncertain. Any time you're climbing at this altitude, there's a danger that some of you could get sick, some could be injured, or possibly even die."

His words hung in the air, a stark reminder of the challenge before us. I looked around at the faces of my fellow climbers, a mix of determination and apprehension. The reality of what we were undertaking settled in, but so did a sense of camaraderie and resolve. This was our adventure, with all its risks and rewards, and we were ready to face it together.

Each step was a lesson in endurance and leadership, much like navigating the highs and lows of a career or managing a team through uncertain times. The climb became tougher as the elevation increased, mirroring the escalating challenges one faces with greater responsibilities. Leadership was not just about reaching the top but about the journey, about managing oneself through the thinning air of high stakes and the cold winds of adversity.

Peter's words from the first day resonated with me as we climbed, each step a mix of determination and trepidation among the group. This climb, much like life's journey, was filled with unknowns, risks, and the potential for great rewards. This shared experience seemed to forge us together; the fellowship and collective resolve grew with each step.

The climb stirred reflections of my professional journey—starting with my leadership role at Ketchum in Chicago, defying my mother's skeptical predictions to Dad and my sisters that I would fail and return home in a year or less, and navigating through the ranks of major public relations firms. Each professional milestone mirrored the physical elevation gained on this mountain.

Over the next decade, I built a strong reputation as an agency leader with Ketchum, Hill & Knowlton, Golin Harris, and Insidedge—the latter an employee engagement firm we created within The Interpublic Group of Companies—and became the recognized authority on employee communication. I had the privilege of serving great brands like IBM, FedEx, Genentech, Boeing, Ford Motor Company, Amazon, ExxonMobil, and American Airlines. Our employee engagement frontline "listening" models proved so effective that we were retained by NASA, the FAA, and NATO to help these massive organizations resolve thorny engagement issues in the US and internationally.

Amid the climb, I thought about my family settled back in Naperville, thriving in a community that contrasted sharply with the desolate mountain trails. Even as we climbed that day, I knew Sue and our daughter, Jordan, were shopping for wedding dresses for Jordie's June wedding, which made me both sad and blissfully happy at the same time. The support and stability we found in the community were my anchor, much like the resolve I felt with each step toward Kilimanjaro's summit.

At one of our brief rests, I looked around at the faces of my fellow climbers. It struck me profoundly that each person's struggle up this mountain was a personal battle, a mirror to the challenges of their individual lives. Peter's insights about leadership and growth during the initial briefing came flooding back. His mentoring had prepared me for both professional leadership and moments like this—understanding that every hardship and every victory on this climb was part of a larger journey.

Looking back, while we would visit our families in Garland during holidays, the gravitational pull of "home" weakened more each year. I spoke less and less with Mom, who ruminated about me being so far away but refused my many offers to fly her to Chicago for visits with our family.

After years of abusing his body, Dad's health began to decline in the '90s. It was discovered that he had prostate cancer, and surgery at the VA Hospital was required to remove his diseased gland. That left him despairing because he no longer could achieve an erection, he told us, which affected his manhood. Then, he had a stroke, from which he recovered over time.

Years later, in October 1995, we faced another challenge. Mom called to tell me she had been diagnosed with breast cancer and was beginning chemotherapy. Sue and I gathered our family and made plans to travel down to Dallas before Halloween. When we arrived, Mom greeted us at the front door wearing a wig. The chemotherapy had taken its toll, and her once-thick black hair was now sparse and brittle. Seeing her like this, trying to maintain a semblance of normalcy, filled us with a deep unease. Mom bounced around the house for two days, giving a performance that portrayed her as being energized and confident, but I knew better. She was very sick.

A few months later, I returned to Dallas and went to see Mom at Baylor Hospital, where she had been admitted for treatment. Her cancer had progressed to Stage 4 and metastasized throughout her body, including her brain. When I entered her room, she was sitting on the bed, her eyes vacant and staring into an unseen distance. I took her hand, its warmth a fragile connection to the woman who had once been my rock.

I whispered to her, "*I love you, Mom,*" my voice trembling with the weight of unspoken fears and regrets. "*I'm so sorry you're going through this.*" But there was no response. The woman I knew, who had always been so full of life, was not there. Her silence was deafening, a stark reminder of the cruel reality that cancer had taken more than just her health.

Tears blurred my vision as I stood there, feeling utterly helpless. I pressed her hand gently, hoping for some sign of recognition, but none came. Overwhelmed by a profound sorrow, I finally let go, my heart breaking as I walked out of her hospital room, leaving a part of myself behind.

Cynthia telephoned the evening of April 18, 1996, to let me know that Mom was near death in a nursing home in Garland. She told me it was time to say my goodbyes. I booked the first flight the next morning and arrived at the facility within hours. As I entered the room, the sight of Mom on a respirator, unconscious and struggling for every breath, hit me like a wave. Her emaciated body lay frail and fragile on the bed, a stark contrast to the vibrant woman I once knew.

I leaned down over her, my heart aching with the reality of her suffering. *"Mom, I'm here,"* I whispered softly into her ear, hoping for any sign of acknowledgment. There was no response, only the rhythmic sound of the respirator. *"I love you, Mom. I want you to know that always. I'm sorry you've had to live your life in pain."*

As I held her hand, memories flooded back—of Little Betty on Gaston Avenue, a mother who cared deeply for her five children despite the chaos that surrounded us. She had endured the dysfunction of an alcoholic husband and the interminable struggles that came with it. Through it all, she remained our steadfast anchor, even when the storm seemed too fierce to weather.

I sat with her for an hour, holding her hand, feeling the warmth that still lingered despite the coldness of impending loss. I remembered her laughter, her strength, and the sacrifices she made for us. Tears streamed down my face as I realized how much she had given and how much she had suffered in silence.

"Mom, you were always there for us, even when it was hardest for you," I whispered, my voice choked with emotion. *"You deserve peace now. You've fought long enough."*

The room was filled with a profound silence, save for the mechanical breaths of the respirator. I felt a deep connection with her in that moment, a love that transcended words and time. As I prepared to leave, I kissed her forehead gently, a final act of love and gratitude. "*Goodbye, Mom,*" I said softly. "*It's time for you to go home now. I love you and will carry you in my heart always.*"

Leaving the nursing home, I felt a mix of sorrow and peace. Sorrow for the pain she had endured and the loss we were facing, but peace knowing that her suffering would soon end. As I walked away, I carried with me the strength and love she had always shown, determined to honor her memory in all that I did.

I returned to the airport and flew home. When I drove into the garage that afternoon, Sue came out to greet me, her eyes filled with tears, a silent reflection of the heartbreak we both felt. She hugged me tightly, her embrace a small refuge from the storm raging inside me. With a voice trembling with emotion, she whispered, "Your sister called. Your mom passed away right after you left."

In that moment, the finality of it all hit me like a tidal wave. She was gone. My heart shattered, and I clung to Sue, seeking solace in her warmth. The realization that Mom had waited until after I left to take her final breath felt like a bittersweet blessing. She had held on for our goodbye, giving me a chance to tell her one last time how much I loved her. As I stood there, wrapped in Sue's arms, I let the tears flow freely, mourning the loss of my mother while holding onto the unwavering love she had instilled in me.

Dad held on for two more years after Mom's passing, but he was merely a shadow of his former self. The vibrancy and vigor that once defined him had faded away, leaving behind a hollow man. He still smoked and drank, but these vices no longer brought him any semblance of joy or escape. Occasionally, he would sell a used car for some spending money; gone, however, were the days when he was celebrated as Salesman of the Month or found camaraderie with bookies, gamblers, and girlfriends. His world had shrunk, his life a mere echo of what it once was.

All that remained was a coop in the backyard, where he housed pigeons. It seemed an odd hobby, but for him, it was a connection to a simpler, happier time. As a boy in Cleburne, he had raised pigeons, training them to fly from the Nolan River back to the family farm. He often reminisced about those simpler days, fishing on the Nolan, feeling the sun on his face, and the joy of a quiet, uncomplicated life. Watching his grandfather work on the windmill at the Burton homestead, he had learned the values of hard work and perseverance. These memories were etched deeply into his soul.

Dad's time as a Marine on the remote atoll of Ulithi had shaped him, instilling a sense of duty and resilience. But the horrors of war had also left scars, ones he never spoke of. The pigeons, in their way, were a return to a time before all that, a bridge to the innocence of his youth.

Now, in the twilight of his life, he returned to this childhood passion, perhaps seeking solace in the familiar. He would carefully tend to his birds, nurturing them as he once did in his youth. Then, he would load them into crates, then into his car, and drive out to the country. There, he would release them, watching as they soared into the sky, finding their way back home. It was a poignant ritual, a symbol of yearning for a lost sense of direction and purpose. The pigeons, with their instinctual drive to return, embodied a hope and a memory of a time when life was simpler and filled with promise.

In those moments, as he watched the pigeons disappear into the horizon, perhaps he found a fleeting sense of peace. It was a reminder of who he once was and a testament to the enduring connection between past and present. The pigeons always came home, a metaphor for his own journey through life, seeking a place of comfort and belonging in a world that had grown increasingly foreign.

He cherished the Burton homestead, a sanctuary of his childhood brimming with memories of family, love, and simpler times. The joy of fishing on the river and the carefree days of youth were his touchstones. These recollections provided comfort and a sense of continuity as he faced the final chapters of his life, clinging to the remnants of a once secure and whole world.

In the final days of his life in February 1998, my sister Charlotte recalled Dad's restlessness and a deep melancholy. His voice, once robust with the enthusiasm of a born salesman, had become weary and despondent. One evening, while driving with Charlotte after dinner, Dad slammed his fist on her dashboard and said, "God can just come take me tonight, as far as I'm concerned! I'm ready to go right now! I have nothing to live for! Nothing interests me anymore!" Those words lingered in the air, heavy with the weight of his surrender.

Two weeks later, his wish was granted. He suffered a heart attack and died alone at home at the age of seventy-four, leaving behind a life that had once been full of promise but now ended in quiet resignation.

It's been said that death ends a life, but it doesn't end a relationship. It struggles along toward resolution in the mind of the survivor. As Charlotte reminded me years later, Dad was never comfortable with his children, with small talk, or with expressing his love and emotions. I never really had a father. He ran away from me, and I ran away from him.

Through all those years, I never remember Dad telling me he loved me. Our relationship was marked by an unspoken distance, a chasm that neither of us could bridge. His inability to connect left a void, and my reaction was to distance myself further. This unresolved tension continues to play out in my memories as I try to understand the complexities of our relationship. His silent presence, more than his words, imprinted a sense of longing and unmet expectations. Even now, I grapple with the emotional impact of that unspoken void, seeking to reconcile the love that was never expressed with the fatherly figure I yearned to understand.

"But even if my father and mother abandon me, the Lord will hold me close" (Psalm 27:10). This scripture brought me solace, reminding me that despite the absence of paternal love, I was never truly alone.

Charlotte's recollection underscores the loneliness Dad must have felt, mirroring my own. His final outburst was a stark expression of his despair, a desperate plea for an end to his suffering. In his passing, I grapple with the remnants of a relationship that never fully formed, struggling to find closure and peace.

The journey toward resolution is ongoing as I reflect on the man he was and the impact he had on my life. His story reminds me of the importance of emotional connection and the profound effect absence can have on those left behind. As I navigate the path of understanding and acceptance, I carry with me the lessons of his life and the shadows of our unresolved bond.

One day, a profound realization washed over me. For years, I had struggled to accept my parents for who they were, often feeling a sense of resentment and confusion. But I was wrong. I came to understand that God chose them specifically because they possessed what was needed to create *me*. My birth was no accident; it was a part of a divine plan. As it says in Jeremiah 29:11, *"'For I know the plans I have for you,' declares the Lord, 'plans to prosper you and not to harm you, plans to give you hope and a future.'"* Everything about it was meticulously orchestrated by God's love. He planned my life with an intentionality that speaks to His immense love for me. Now, with this newfound understanding, I feel a deep desire to express that love back, honoring the purpose and the journey He set forth for me. This realization has transformed my perspective, turning pain into gratitude and guiding me toward a deeper, more meaningful connection with my faith and my family.

My thoughts returned to our final ascent to the summit of Mount Kilimanjaro. It was 11 p.m. on Day Four, and after a fitful two hours of lying in my upper bunk, our team was rousted up to dress in our warmest gear. It was go time! The guides' voices cut through the cold night air, a stark reminder of the grueling challenge that lay ahead. This final push to the summit was shrouded in an almost palpable sense of anticipation and dread.

The climb over the next six hours of Day Five would be the most mentally and physically challenging portion of the trek. The wind howled mercilessly, biting through layers of clothing and chilling us to the bone. Snow began to fall, driven like tiny daggers by the wind. The cold at this elevation was a formidable enemy, seeking to sap our strength and resolve. The darkness enveloped us, broken only by the faint, flickering beams of our headlamps.

We ascended at a slow, methodical pace, each step a battle against the thin air and relentless elements. The path wound steeply upwards, a seemingly endless series of switchbacks. Our breaths came in ragged gasps, each one a reminder of the altitude's unforgiving grip. The only sounds were the crunch of our boots on the frozen scree and the occasional murmur of encouragement from our guides.

The hours stretched on, feeling like an eternity. Every few minutes, we took brief, desperately needed breaks, huddling together to shield ourselves from the icy wind. Our muscles ached, and exhaustion threatened to overtake us, but the promise of the summit kept us moving forward. The darkness seemed impenetrable; a vast, cold void that made the summit feel impossibly far away.

Yet, with each step, we were closer to our goal. The air grew thinner, the wind colder, and the climb steeper, but our determination burned bright. We were driven by the hope of reaching the top, of standing on the roof of Africa as the first light of dawn broke over the horizon.

As the minutes turned to hours, the faintest hint of a glow began to appear on the horizon, signaling the approaching sunrise. It was a beacon of hope, a promise that the summit was near. With renewed vigor, we pushed on, every muscle screaming in protest, but our spirits unyielding. The summit was within our grasp, and nothing would stop us from reaching it.

Accompanied by our guide, Edward Ernest Kutingala, a Tanzanian who hailed from Arusha, I arrived at Gilman's Point at 18,600 feet around 5:30 a.m., and we were rewarded with the most magnificent sunrise you are ever likely to see coming over Mawenzi Peak. The horizon burst into a kaleidoscope of colors, painting the sky with hues of orange, pink, and gold. I took a deep breath, feeling the thin air fill my lungs, and rested briefly before climbing up to the rim of Kili and heading on toward the final summit.

After trudging slowly around the rim for what seemed like an eternity, I arrived at Uhuru Peak—elevation 19,340 feet, the highest point on Mount Kilimanjaro and the continent of Africa. The narrow path along the edge was dizzying, and every glance down into the caldera of the long-dormant volcano filled me with a vertiginous fear. The vast, yawning chasm below was a stark reminder of the mountain's ancient and powerful past.

Shafts of morning sunlight pierced the crystal-clear sky. I let out a triumphant yell and grabbed Ernest for a hug. *"We did it, Ernest! Thank you for helping me every step of the way!"*

Nearby, I heard the voice of Peter, my friend and life guide. He climbed over to where we stood and gathered several of our group for a photo in front of the sign proclaiming it the highest point in Africa. Then he turned to me and said, *"Well done, friend! Well done!"* I looked into his eyes and saw the genuine joy he felt for me and the team he had led up the mountain.

I knew Peter more intimately than anyone on our trip. I first met him in 1993 when I attended the Leadership Development Program offered by the Center for Creative Leadership in St. Petersburg, Florida. At the time, I was struggling in my role as general manager of Ketchum. I had enrolled in this program with twenty-five other senior professionals from across the United States—bankers, CFOs, CMOs, consultants, full-bird colonels preparing to become one-star generals, and the manager of the largest nuclear power plant in America. Our purpose as a cohort was to discover the truth of our leadership.

Peter was my LDP program advisor, providing deeper insights into my strengths and weaknesses than anyone I had ever encountered. He meticulously analyzed the 360-degree reviews conducted with my colleagues at Ketchum, revealing profound truths I needed to hear. "Feedback is a gift," he told me. "You may not always like it, but the people who gave it to you care and want you to be a better leader."

He had a unique ability to probe the depths of my successes and failures, bringing clarity and truth to the surface. He used stories to illustrate how we can build on our strengths and recognize our blind spots. His words cut through the noise, reaching the core of my being, and ignited a spark of self-awareness and growth.

Peter's guidance shaped my approach to leadership and personal development. Standing on the summit of Kilimanjaro, with the world stretched out below us and the dawn of a new day breaking over the horizon, I felt a deep sense of accomplishment and clarity. The climb was more than a physical challenge; it was a metaphor for the journey of life, filled with trials, revelations, and the unwavering support of those who guide us.

As the morning sun bathed the landscape in golden light, my mother's words echoed in my mind: "Remember, it's about the journey, not the destination." Those words, once a gentle reminder in my youth, now resonated with profound truth. Life's most valuable lessons are learned along the way, through the struggles and triumphs, setbacks and breakthroughs.

I realized that every step we take, every obstacle we overcome, and every lesson we learn is part of a greater journey. It's about resilience, determination, and the courage to face our inner demons. It's about the people who stand by us, offering wisdom and encouragement when we falter. On that mountaintop, I embraced the lessons Peter had imparted and the wisdom my mother had instilled in me.

True leadership is not just about success but about learning from our failures and rising stronger. It's about being open to feedback, valuing the perspectives of others, and continually striving to be better. The climb to Kilimanjaro's summit was a testament to the power of perseverance and the transformative impact of insightful guidance.

As I stood there, with the vast expanse of Africa below and the promise of a new day ahead, I understood that the journey truly defines us. It reminded me that with the right support, we can reach unimaginable heights. The climb, with all its challenges and triumphs, was not just about reaching the summit; it was about every moment, every struggle, every shared laugh and tear along the way.

Inspired by my mother's wisdom and Peter's guidance, I vowed to carry these lessons forward. To honor the journey, to embrace each step, and to lead with the knowledge that it's the path we walk, not just the peak we reach, that shapes who we are. In that moment of clarity, I felt a profound connection to my purpose, ready to face whatever lay ahead with courage, humility, and an unwavering spirit.

CHAPTER 14

The Weight of Unheard Voices

In 2010, I embarked on a project with ExxonMobil, one of the world's largest publicly held international oil and gas companies, to address communication issues at its Torrance, California, refinery. Opened in 1929, this facility was rich in history and tradition, yet it had become a crucible for a broken culture. Our task was to diagnose the roots of these communication challenges and create a "blueprint" to help executives improve effectiveness and unity among the workforce.

For those who worked at the Torrance refinery, the sense of history was palpable. Many front-line managers and hourly employees had called it home for decades, often spending twenty, thirty, or even forty years on its grounds. As I walked through the facility, where we interviewed more than one hundred fifty executives, managers, and hourly workers over several weeks, employees shared their stories and pride, echoing sentiments like, "Our careers are here, not somewhere else," and "This is my home!" Pegasus Park, adorned with the iconic red Pegasus—the heritage symbol of Mobil—stood as a silent reminder of an era that many employees cherished. The winged horse, a symbol of speed, power, and freedom, evoked memories of the company's storied past. Some employees, in quiet defiance, still wore their Mobil uniforms a decade after ExxonMobil emerged as its successor, holding on to the legacy that Pegasus represented.

However, beneath this pride lay uncertainty and concern for the refinery's future. With the petroleum refining industry in decline, whispers circulated about what might happen next. Employees wondered if the Torrance unit would be sold, become a gateway for processing crude from tankers in the South Bay, or merely serve as a tank farm for California's fuel products. They longed for the golden days of peak gasoline demand and high prices when the refinery operated at optimal output and safety. Back then, bonuses and recognition for a job well done were not just appreciated; they were expected.

The divide between Heritage Exxon and Heritage Mobil ran deep, affecting daily operations. For front-line managers, the emphasis on safety, reliability, and profitability was both a challenge and a source of pride. However, they struggled with the refinery's focus on engineering precision over innovation and "intrapreneurship." The revolving door of executive leaders, who often viewed their roles as mere steps on a career ladder, left managers feeling unsupported and hourly employees feeling overlooked.

Front-line managers and hourly employees sought accomplishment, mentorship, and trust from their leaders but often faced unclear directives and a lack of context for their work. The absence of accountability in communications and engagement only exacerbated their frustration. They craved clear communication and genuine engagement from their superiors, not just directives handed down from above.

"Is anyone listening?" This mantra, long voiced by Gary Grates, a cherished colleague and true innovator in employee engagement, echoed a challenge frequently heard among the workforce. Employees pointed to past meetings with leaders in which their feedback was documented but then abandoned, left to languish on conference room tables or in metaphorical "parking lots." Change was constant, yet meaningful progress seemed elusive.

One day, as I sat preparing to lead a focus group at the refinery, my mind drifted back to an earlier time in my life when I, too, wondered, "Is anyone listening?"

Dad had promised to take me to watch the Harlem Globetrotters play their perennial opponents, the Washington Generals, in Dallas, and I was ecstatic. I loved basketball and was a huge fan of the Globetrotters. Whenever they were on television, I watched every minute, captivated by the antics of Meadowlark Lemon, "Curly" Neal, and Marques Haynes. Their skill and humor on the court were magical to me, and the thought of seeing them live filled me with excitement.

For weeks, I counted down the days, telling my friends I was finally going to see the storied Globetrotters in action. As game day approached, my anticipation reached a fever pitch. Late that afternoon, I dressed carefully, choosing my favorite outfit for the special occasion. I sat by the front window, eyes fixed on the driveway, waiting eagerly for Dad's arrival, imagining the laughter and cheers that awaited us at the arena.

As the hours passed and the time for the game drew near, the light outside dimmed, and so did my hope. Dad didn't show up. The silence was deafening, each tick of the clock a reminder of yet another broken promise. I was left sitting there, heartbroken and confused, grappling with the crushing disappointment. The excitement that had filled my heart was replaced by a deep sense of not being valued. I felt invisible, my hopes dashed, and my trust shaken. In that moment, I realized how fragile the promise of connection could be when built on empty words. I always had the feeling he didn't really want to be with me, a quiet certainty that settled into my bones over the years.

Dad was someone who wanted to look good without doing good, making empty promises to appear reliable while failing to follow through. He perfected the art of lying, and when you questioned why he was untruthful, he would make you believe you were wrong. "I'm really sorry," he would say. "Something came up last night. I got busy and couldn't leave. I'll make it up to you, I promise." But those promises were as insubstantial as smoke, dissipating the moment they were made.

When you sit across from a loved one to engage in a heartfelt, intimate conversation, you expect eye contact and a real connection. Dad could never look you in the eye. He would look off to his right while he spoke to you, his words empty and hollow. The conversations were always brief, their connection superficial and insincere. His inability to engage left a void that words could not fill, a reminder of the emotional distance that seemed insurmountable.

This pattern played out every major holiday, at Boy Scout meetings, at games in which I played, or during school events. The routine was the same: grand promises followed by silence and absence, leaving me to pick up the pieces of my disappointment alone. In the wake of these crushing blows, Mom would always say the same thing: "What can I say? It's your dad, and you should know what to expect…" Her words were a reminder of the resignation that had settled into our lives, a quiet acceptance of Dad's inability to truly be there.

I remember when I broke my wrist sliding into second base in an all-star game. The crack of bone was sharp, echoing my own internal fracture as I realized Dad was nowhere to be found. Mom was off ferrying the girls to their activities and caring for Kurtis. Coach McCartney had to load me into the back of his station wagon and haul me over to the Garland Clinic & Hospital for treatment. Lying in that sterile room, I felt a profound loneliness, wishing for a comforting presence that never came.

When I finally saw Dad two days later, he came into my room, patted me on the head, and said, "Sorry that happened, pal," and then left for work without even asking about the game. His words were a hollow echo, devoid of empathy or understanding. He had no time for love or emotions. Even when his own mother was hospitalized with terminal colon cancer and asked to see him a final time before her painful death,

Dad was nowhere to be found. His absence in those moments spoke louder than any words, a testament to the emotional distance that defined our relationship.

Years later, Dad invited me to join him and a coworker for an overnight fishing trip. I knew this would mean a night of heavy drinking, cursing, and horseplay for these men on the boat. I remember drifting off to sleep in the pre-dawn hours, waking up, and hearing Dad talking about me to his friend. "Yeah, that kid is hung like a horse," he said of me. My dad, who didn't know or love me after all these years, used me to validate his own manhood and hurt me deeply with this crude description of who I was as his beloved son.

There's a video of a 16-mm film from the 1933 reunion of the Burton family, a cherished relic from a bygone era. It was held at Granddaddy A.T. Burton, Sr.'s farm in Cleburne—the homestead that Dad adored. The footage captures my grandfathers, grandmothers, aunts, and uncles basking in the joy of a halcyon afternoon on the vast Texas prairie, their laughter mingling with the gentle breeze. Children played in a swimming pool, their carefree splashes punctuating the scene with bursts of youthful exuberance.

There was Dad, nine years old, beaming in the golden glow of the late afternoon sun, his smile wide and unguarded. I wondered what he was thinking that day, lost in the innocence of his young life. Did he dream of adventures yet to come? Did he feel the warmth of love and belonging that so often eluded him later in life?

Watching the film, I couldn't help but feel a pang of longing for that little boy with sun-bleached hair—before time etched its complexities into his heart, before promises were broken and connections left unmade. It was a poignant reminder of the simplicity and purity that once existed, a glimpse into a moment when everything seemed possible. In that fleeting image, I saw not just my father but the hope and joy of a child untouched by the burdens of the world.

Dad's inability to truly connect with those who loved him haunted his legacy. I have a letter from his Aunt Margie Stewart, his mother's sister, who could never understand why Dad closed the door on his family in Cleburne. When Grandaddy A.T. Burton died, Aunt Margie wanted to fly to Dallas for the funeral. Dad discouraged it by calling her and saying, "Since Daddy was so old and most people had forgotten him, or were deceased, graveside services will be held immediately and there's no reason for you to come." This left his beloved aunt deeply offended.

Reflecting on these memories, I understood the yearning of the employees at the refinery. Their desire to be heard and respected mirrored my own childhood longing. Too often, people want to look good without doing good, making promises that ring hollow. It became clear that listening and keeping promises were not just acts of kindness; they were vital to building trust and fostering a sense of belonging. As I prepared to lead work that would help bridge the communication gap at the refinery, I was determined to ensure that every voice would be heard and every promise would be honored.

Power is not sufficient evidence of truth. This realization has unfolded countless times throughout history and in the quiet corners of our personal lives. Growing up, I often witnessed the influence of power—how it could bend reality, shape narratives, and overshadow the actual truth.

In my family, power was wielded like a scepter, its authority unquestioned and its presence all-encompassing. My father, despite his faults, carried a certain power. He had the ability to command a room, to make his voice the loudest, to convince those around him that he held the answers. Yet beneath the surface of his imposing presence, the truth was often more complex and sometimes painfully absent.

I learned early on that power can create an illusion of truth, a facade that hides vulnerabilities and failures. My father's promises, made with such conviction, were part of that illusion. They seemed powerful and true at the moment, but too often, they crumbled under the weight of reality. He could make you believe in the strength of his words, even as the truth remained elusive.

This understanding extended beyond my family, resonating in the world around me. I saw how power could dictate what was accepted as truth and how those in positions of authority could shape the narrative to suit their needs. But I also saw the cracks in that facade, where truth struggled to break free, persistent and unyielding.

In my work at the Torrance refinery, I came to value the quiet power of truth over the loud declarations of authority. I realized that true connection and progress stem from listening, understanding, and honoring the realities of others, rather than imposing one's own version of the truth. It taught me that real power lies in vulnerability, in the courage to confront uncomfortable truths, and in the willingness to bridge gaps and build trust.

Power may influence perception, but it is not the arbiter of truth. Truth, in its purest form, stands independent of power's reach. It is found in the honest exchanges between people, in the shared understanding of our experiences, and in the authenticity of our actions. It taught me that the real strength comes from acknowledging the truth, even when it challenges the foundations of power.

As we worked to develop a more effective communication strategy, it became clear that addressing these concerns was crucial. Front-line managers and hourly employees wanted to be heard and valued, and they deserved a culture where actions matched words. By fostering an environment where every voice mattered, the Torrance Refinery could hope to reclaim its former glory and move confidently into the future. Through our efforts, we aimed to bridge the gap between management and the workforce, ensuring that the rich legacy of the refinery continued with renewed purpose and commitment.

In the end, however, the weight of unheard voices came crashing down on the Torrance refinery, nestled in the heart of a community of 150,000 people. On February 18, 2015, a catastrophic explosion resulted from unsafe alternative procedures implemented during maintenance, causing severe property damage and scattering toxic catalyst dust over a mile into the surrounding area. The dust posed unknown long-term health risks to the residents. The refinery was forced to operate at limited capacity for over a year, driving up gasoline prices across California and reportedly costing drivers an estimated $2.4 billion.

An investigation by the U.S. Chemical Safety Board (CSB), an independent, non-regulatory federal agency charged with investigating serious chemical incidents, revealed that refinery managers had ignored clear danger signs and used expired equipment, violating three of Chevron Phillips' 10 Tenets of Operation. This pursuit of maximizing gasoline production and profit backfired, leading to four worker injuries, a $566,000 fine from OSHA, and a significant hit to the company's stock.

Under regulatory scrutiny, ExxonMobil ultimately sold the crippled plant for $537.5 million to independent refiner PBF Energy. The incident underscored the critical importance of adhering to safety protocols and the ethical principles that ensure a safer and more profitable work environment.

Reflecting on the parallels between my personal experiences and the challenges faced at the Torrance refinery, I realized that the core issues shared a common thread: the importance of listening, the impact of broken promises, and the need for transparency and accountability. My father's inability to keep promises left me with a longing for connection and trust, a sentiment echoed by the workers who felt their voices were not being heard.

Proverbs 31:8-9 reminds us to "speak up for those who cannot speak for themselves" and to "defend the rights of the poor and needy." These verses call us to be active listeners and advocates, ensuring that every voice is heard and respected. They challenge us to create environments where justice and fairness prevail, guiding our actions with empathy and integrity.

The events at the Torrance refinery highlighted the necessity of prioritizing communication and safety in any organization. By focusing on these values, companies can foster an environment of trust and collaboration, benefiting both the workforce and the broader community.

As I continue my journey, the wisdom of Proverbs 31:8-9 serves as a guiding light, inspiring me to advocate for a culture where listening and ethical actions lead to positive change. The weight of unheard voices can be a catalyst for transformation, underscoring the power of empathy and the importance of acting with care and responsibility.

CHAPTER 15

A Decade of Adventures: Rediscovering Love and Life

In 2013, I returned home from a thrilling rafting trip in Alaska with Peter and a group of outdoorsmen to find a wooden block inscribed with the words "I want to have adventures with you" on our kitchen counter in Naperville. Sue had left it there for me to discover. Having traveled forty-eight out of fifty-two weeks that year in my work as a partner with London-based Brunswick Group, a communications consultancy, it was a wake-up call. The message was clear: It was time to slow down and prioritize my schedule for one purpose—to spend quality time with the love of my life.

That simple wooden block symbolized a pivotal moment in our lives. It marked the transition from a relentless work and travel schedule, which I had maintained for years, to a life enriched with shared experiences and adventures. For the past decade, Sue and I have journeyed together around the globe, creating cherished memories and deepening our bond. This wooden block stands as a testament to our commitment to embracing life's adventures and prioritizing our relationship above every earthly concern, with Christ as our first priority.

We've traveled in the UK and France, strolling through Hyde Park, touring the Tower of London, the Westminster Cathedral, and the Churchill War Museum. We've also visited Monet's home in Giverny and the champagne region in Hautvillers and Èperney, and toured the magnificent Notre Dame, Chartres, and Reims cathedrals.

As oenophiles, we've made numerous trips to Napa and Sonoma, California, and the Willamette Valley of Oregon, where we've hiked, enjoyed vineyard tours, savored fine dining, and indulged in great wines.

Our shared love of the outdoors has led us on hiking trips to Starved Rock and Matthiessen State Parks in Illinois, and Devil's Head State Park in Wisconsin. We've also embarked on outdoor adventures in Scottsdale and Sedona, Arizona; Palm Desert and Joshua Tree National Park in California; Bend, Sisters, and Crater Lake National Park in Oregon; and the Black Hills, the Badlands, and Mount Rushmore in South Dakota.

In August 2024, we celebrated our forty-seventh wedding anniversary, a testament to our enduring love and partnership.

Our lives together have not been without challenges. In December 2022, Sue was walking Murphy, our wonderful golden retriever, on a quiet Sunday afternoon, when she suddenly felt dizzy. With Murphy's guidance and support, she made her way off the prairie path and back to our neighborhood, where she collapsed in the parkway not far from our home.

A neighbor leaving her driveway spotted Sue and pulled over immediately. She raced over and asked, "Are you in trouble?"

"I think I am," Sue told her. The neighbor, a cardiac care nurse at nearby Northwestern Delnor Hospital, was ready to dial 911 when Sue asked her to run Murphy back home and bring me outside to join her. Within minutes of our call, an ambulance arrived, and medical technicians went to work on my wife.

At the hospital, we learned that Sue had suffered a STEMI (ST-Segment Elevation Myocardial Infarction), the most severe type of heart attack. This occurs when an artery supplying blood to the heart becomes partially or completely blocked by a blood clot. As she awaited intervention in the emergency room, her cardiologist informed her of the heart attack. For a woman who looks twenty years her junior and prides herself on maintaining a healthy diet, exercising actively, and taking care of her health, Sue was puzzled. In her inimitable style and humor, she said, *"Are you talking to me? I didn't have a heart attack! I think you're in the wrong room!"*

We would later learn that women, unlike men, don't experience the classic chest pains. Instead, they may become dizzy, as was the case for my wife.

Clot-busting drugs were administered, and two stents were placed in her coronary arteries. Four days later, she was back home. By the grace of God, she had no damage to her heart and has fully recovered. Sue now has a pacemaker, a small device implanted under the skin near the heart, to help control abnormal heart rhythms. She's living the active lifestyle we've always enjoyed together, and we continue to travel and hike throughout the United States. Praise God for His blessings and mercy!

My thoughts returned to a former trustee of the Institute for Public Relations with whom I served for many years. He was the communications head for a major utility company, based in both Washington, DC, and on the Gulf Coast. As he neared retirement after a distinguished career, I asked him what he planned to do next. "I'm a Civil War aficionado. When I'm done in a few months, I'll hit the road to visit all the battlefields and memorials I've always wanted to see," he said with a gleam in his eye.

But within days of his formal retirement, this gentle and considerate leader suffered a massive stroke and never left his bed again. He was dead in less than a year.

Then there was Al Golin, my mentor and founder of the public relations agency that bears his name. One day, he received a note from a former client executive asking if he could drop by the office for a visit. Al agreed, and at the appointed hour, his guest arrived. Al greeted the man and took him back to his office. They engaged in the usual chitchat expected when two friends who have grown apart reunite. After about forty-five minutes, the man looked at his watch, patted his leg, and stood up, his hand outstretched. "Al, thank you for seeing me. I wish you the very best." Then he departed.

A week later, Al read in the *Chicago Tribune* that his guest had died. I asked him what he thought about it, and he said, "Unfinished business."

Never take life for granted. Never waste a day. Never let pass the opportunity to tell the one you love how much they mean to you.

It took me back to a time twenty years earlier when I was on a flight to Asia. In my diary, I wrote the following:

> American Airlines Flight 153, over Anchorage, Alaska; Sunday, June 22, 2003
>
> *We are en route to Tokyo today. From there, four more hours of waiting; then four more hours of flight to Hong Kong.*
>
> *In these moments of reflection, the lessons of life become even clearer. I've always had everything I want and need in my life, though I haven't always known this in my heart. Sue is the partner God always intended for me. She has an incredible capacity to love others, to be humble and charitable. Sometimes, I find myself lost in anger, perhaps because I've been too self-absorbed.*
>
> *It's been a long sleepwalk. I'm missing out on the true gifts God has given to me.*
>
> **Gift one:** *My life. Rather than living in the moment, I've been living in the past or for tomorrow. Live for now! Enjoy each moment! Give thanks to God the Father!*

Gift two: *The blessings of life. To be alive. To have my health and well-being. To have the abundance God has given me. The gift of freedom, of love, of faith. These are the true riches of the world. I'm truly blessed!*

Gift three: *My children. I love them. As they age and mature, I love them as they grow, stretch, experience new things, and meet the challenge of becoming adults.*

My prayer: *I'm grateful for my life. May I live it confidently and boldly in faith. May I open myself fully to the blessings before me. May I cherish and honor my loving wife and partner. May I be the father that my children need.*

In Jesus' Blessed Name I pray, Amen.

As Sue and I hiked through the stunning landscapes of the Black Hills of South Dakota in 2023, I couldn't help but reflect on her simple act a decade earlier—placing that inscribed block on the counter for me to find. Surely inspired by our Lord, it served as a profound stop sign in my life, halting my relentless work schedule and refocusing my priorities. *"Commit your way to the Lord; trust in Him, and He will act"* (Psalm 37:5). That small, wooden block brought me back to the one person who means more than anything in this world, transforming our journey and deepening our bond in ways I never imagined.

Our adventures have ranged from the exhilarating to the serene. We've biked mountain roads, navigated remote trails hewn from abandoned railways, hiked majestic peaks, picnicked by serene mountain lakes, and explored vibrant cities. Each journey has been a chapter in our lives, filled with laughter, discovery, and love. Sue has been my constant companion and loving partner. These moments, big and small, have woven the tapestry of our life together, each thread representing a shared experience and a deepening of our love.

As we walked hand-in-hand through Mount Rushmore National Park, I reminded my loving wife how that small gesture, inspired by divine guidance, set us on a path of deeper connection and shared joy. It's a path we continue to walk together, grateful for every moment, every adventure, and every day we have with each other.

Our adventures have taught us that life is not just about the destinations but the journey we take together. Each step, each mile, and each adventure has brought us closer and made us appreciate the simple, profound gift of being together. Here's to many more years of adventures, with hearts full of love and gratitude for the incredible journey we're on together!

CHAPTER 16

Beneath the Smiles

until i was twenty-two
i didn't think anyone else
had a drunk for a mother
then i met lori joannie and susan
i recognized them immediately
by their stay away smiles
they were leaders in their work
competent imposters
like me
who would say they were sorry
if somebody bumped into them
on a crowded street
i call on them
once in a while
they always come
children of alcoholics
always do

— Jane, adult child, "Daughters of the Bottle"
Taken from *It Will Never Happen to Me* by Claudia Black, PhD

Growing up, the sounds of violent arguments were as familiar as the ticking of the clock in our den. Each of my siblings and I navigated the chaos of our household in different ways, each path marked by the shadows cast by our father's alcoholism. I often wonder how our lives would have been different if our home had been a haven of peace like those of our neighbors—the Sewalls, the Wiggs, the Pruitts, or the Johnsons—instead of a battlefield of unspoken pain. The scars we carry are invisible to the world, but they are etched deeply into our hearts. My sister Charlotte once told me, "We all have our own way of coping, but the truth is, none of us escaped unscathed."

To my siblings—Carol, Cynthia, Charlotte, and Kurtis—you endured the same storms and shouldered the same burdens, though we each faced them during different acts of this tragic play. No one else knows the sorrow, struggle, and strife we experienced like we do. No one else knows the secrets we kept to protect each other. We navigated this journey together, and my greatest regret is that we were never truly brothers and sisters. We were survivors.

As I look back on those years, I see how each of us was shaped by the turbulence and how the dysfunction forged and fractured our paths. This chapter is a journey through those memories, a reflection on the resilience we found amidst the wreckage, and an acknowledgment of the wounds that never fully healed. My intention here is not to judge, but to share the stories as I lived and perceived them, knowing that each of us carries our own truths.

Carol's Journey:

Linda Carol Burton, the sister I loved as a child, changed after leaving home as a teenager. Giving up her son at birth left a lasting mark on her, and life became a series of struggles I didn't fully understand at the time. Now, I see them as rooted in a deep sense of loss, and perhaps betrayal. Yet, despite everything, Carol was the first in our family to graduate from college, earning a degree in education from Texas Wesleyan University—an achievement I admire, considering the challenges she faced.

As a girl, Carol had an undeniable magnetism. She was beautiful, popular, and always seemed to have the latest fashion, the latest everything. But beneath that confidence, I believe she carried burdens none of us could fully comprehend. Over time, her pain manifested as anger, especially toward Mom. Their relationship was fraught with tension, a reflection of unresolved issues Carol carried from those early years.

Her search for stability often played out in her marriages, each one a fresh hope for happiness. But the past followed her, and the anger she carried made it difficult to find peace. Family gatherings could be a mix of her charm and wit, but also moments of sharpness. Her anger often surfaced in painful confrontations with Mom, which were difficult for all of us—especially for Carol, who seemed trapped by emotions she couldn't fully express.

A memory that lingers is the day we buried Mom. Before the final spade of dirt had settled over the grave, Carol began criticizing her, speaking harshly in front of Dad and anyone nearby. It was a heartbreaking moment that laid bare the depth of Carol's unresolved anger—a pain she could never fully release. Even in death, the wounds between them remained unhealed.

Yet, despite her personal turmoil, there were moments of light. Carol found purpose in her work as a teacher, dedicating over thirty years to shaping young minds. She often went above and beyond for her students, ensuring they received not just an education, but also care and attention. This ability to give, even when she was struggling, is something I deeply admire.

Carol was also a devoted mother to her children, Shawn and Edward. She raised them with love, care, and strength, bringing light to their lives as she did with her students. Despite everything, Carol's generosity of spirit was undeniable.

Beneath her anger, I believe there was a sadness she never acknowledged, rooted in the loss of the bond we once shared. For a long time, she didn't remember the little boy who worshipped her, who waited by the window in tears when she left without explanation. That little boy was me.

But years later, something shifted. One September afternoon in her San Antonio kitchen, we found peace. I told her how deeply her absence had affected me, and in that moment, we hugged and cried, letting years of hurt melt away. It wasn't perfect, but it was enough. We had finally bridged the distance that had separated us for so long.

Today, she's Callie Sinclair—Callie, the name Mimmie loved to call her, and Sinclair, her third married name. It suits her now, a mix of past and present, carrying both the weight of who she's been and the search for who she still hopes to become. One day, she looked at Facebook photos of Sue and me hiking, our faces glowing from the fresh air and the sense of freedom that comes from walking a path without the burden of yesterday's weight. She responded, "You're traveling in time to a journey where one can think. Peacefully moving with each other…I'm stuck here with three memories trying to figure out who I am."

Those three memories are of three marriages that didn't work—each one leaving behind fragments of who she once was. They linger like unanswered questions, echoes of hope turned to disappointment, love that somehow slipped through her fingers. While Sue and I walk through nature, free and unburdened, Callie remains tethered to the past, trapped in a loop of "what-ifs" and "could-have-beens," wondering if she'll ever find the sense of self that feels whole again.

Her words, so simple yet profound, struck me deeply. There was an ache in them, a longing for the kind of journey she saw in that picture—one where you're not just walking but finding yourself along the way. She's still on that path, just not yet sure which direction leads to the peace we all hope to find. The weight of those memories is heavy, and I wish I could carry some of it for her, even if just for a while, so that she, too, could move forward, untethered and free.

Cynthia's Journey:

I knew my sister, Cynthia Susan Burton, better than anyone in our family. We were close in age and shared a bedroom growing up. Cynthia was always quiet but sure to have an opinion or a point of view. Many days, it felt like she was the forgotten child, wedged between Carol, the firstborn who was fawned over and favored, and me, the first son. Cynthia's quiet nature, though, belied an inner world filled with music, books, and dreams that perhaps only she fully understood.

Cynthia became a huge fan of the Beatles when the Fab Four burst onto the scene in the early '60s. I can still hear the music blaring from our shared stereo, her joy and excitement contagious. Those were some of the happier days, when music and shared experiences brought us closer together.

But there was a side to Cynthia that was harder to see, a side she kept hidden from most of us. She was a master of masking her pain with a quiet charm that made her seem distant and reserved. Her struggles, particularly with relationships and alcohol, were often kept behind closed doors. Cynthia was married twice—the first union ending when her husband caught her in their home with another man. It was a moment that revealed the complexity of her personal life, which she rarely spoke about. Her relationships often mirrored the inner turmoil she carried, rooted in the scars left by our tumultuous childhood.

Writing about Cynthia is particularly challenging. Her life was marked by so many secrets and private battles that I often wonder if I truly understood her at all. She was fiercely independent, and that independence sometimes came at a cost. There were moments of deception, of broken trust, that cast long shadows over our relationship.

Yet, I know that behind those actions was a woman who was simply trying to survive the only way she knew how.

One particularly difficult memory is the time she took $10,000 from our parents' estate to take her daughter to Disney World without considering her siblings, who were joint heirs. It was a moment that caused tension and resentment within our family, but looking back, I see it as part of the survival instincts many children of alcoholics develop—focusing on immediate needs without considering long-term consequences or the feelings of others. This behavior was deeply hurtful and further fractured our fragile family relationships.

Despite these challenges, Cynthia's later years were marked by a quiet grace. She fought a brave battle against breast cancer that metastasized and ravaged her body, maintaining her dignity and humor until the very end. In those final days, surrounded by her daughter and grandchildren, I believe she found some measure of peace. She is buried next to Mom and Dad in Restland Cemetery, where the Burtons, McCurrys, and Jennings lie in rest. It is a bittersweet comfort to know that she is now at peace, free from the struggles that marked her life.

Charlotte's Journey:

Of all my sisters, Charlotte Jean Burton showed the most promise from the day she was born. She was a beautiful child with a warm smile and long, flowing brown hair that cascaded in curls. She exuded boundless energy. Her green eyes sparkled with curiosity and mischief, drawing people in effortlessly. She was Dad's girl. When he was home, he doted on her, ensuring her every wish was fulfilled. Her laughter filled our house, a bright and vibrant presence that lifted everyone's spirits. In her early years, everyone adored her, captivated by her charm and vivacity.

However, Dad's frequent absences and the tumultuous relationship between him and Mom began to erode her innocence and confidence. The constant fights and emotional strain took a toll on her, dimming the light that once shone so brightly in her eyes. The warmth of her smile became rarer, replaced by a guarded expression that spoke of hurt and disillusionment. The energy that once seemed limitless became tinged with a sense of weariness and skepticism. Charlotte's natural beauty and charm remained, but there was now a layer of sadness and complexity that hadn't been there before. The loving and carefree girl transformed into someone who carried the weight of our family's dysfunction, her promise overshadowed by the harsh realities of our upbringing. In the dark days of discord, she would retreat under the kitchen table and silently pull clumps of hair from her head, forcing Mom to dress her in a winter hat—even in summer.

Her journey was perhaps the most complex for me to understand. As her older brother, I saw her through the eyes of a protector, yet I often felt helpless in shielding her from the pain that shaped her life. My reflections on her life are deeply personal, rooted in the love and frustration I felt as I watched her navigate her own path. Despite the traumatic experiences and the co-dependency that ensnared her, Charlotte managed to find a sense of independence later in life. Her journey reflects the resilience and determination to overcome her past, often seen in children of alcoholics who excel in their professional lives but struggle privately.

When Charlotte was six, she contracted Fifth Disease, known for the bright red "slapped cheek" rash it causes. The rash spread to her arms, legs, and trunk and lasted for weeks. Despite the discomfort and embarrassment, I remember she faced it with remarkable resilience. Her energy, though dampened by our family's turmoil, never fully extinguished. Her experience with the illness was just another layer in the complex tapestry of her young life, a testament to her enduring spirit.

She was sexually molested by a trusted family doctor and again by a teenager in our neighborhood, and never recovered from the mental anguish. She spiraled down through a series of illnesses and often befriended people of questionable character and reputation, one example being when she joined Al-Anon not because she had a drinking problem but because she believed she could make new friends more easily. I remember her dating an older man who was easily sixty when she was in her twenties.

Charlotte married and divorced because of incompatibility. She never had children.

Like Cynthia and, to a lesser degree, me, Charlotte was ensnared by Mom's co-dependency. She lived at home until Mom died and struggled for many years to find her own pathway. Charlotte had a burning desire to be loved, a yearning that stemmed from never truly knowing affection as a child. She bent over backward to care for others, always going the extra mile in hopes of earning their approval. Her gestures were often extravagant and unnecessary, as she spent tens of thousands of dollars from a legal settlement lavishly or wastefully in a desperate bid for acceptance. This relentless pursuit of validation was rooted in the deep-seated void left by our tumultuous upbringing. Charlotte's efforts, though well-meaning, poignantly reflected her unfulfilled need for love and recognition.

Today, Charlotte has achieved a sense of independence, but she remains deeply unsettled. Restlessness and uncertainty persist, reflecting unresolved conflicts from her past. This inner turbulence makes her susceptible to family members who, driven by their own interests, may take advantage of her generosity and financial resources. As scripture reminds us, *"The Lord sees everything you do, and he watches where you go"* (Proverbs 5:21), a reminder that nothing goes unnoticed.

But what about my brother, Kurtis?

Born in 1963, Kurtis arrived during a time when our family's dysfunction was beginning to fade into the background. Dad was increasingly absent, spending more time with his second family in McKinney. While the atmosphere at home wasn't serene, it was no longer as volatile or combative as it had been for many years. I believe that God chose to bless and protect Kurtis for his call to the ministry, even before he was born.

Unlike the rest of us, Kurtis was spared the brunt of the chaos. Perhaps it was divine intervention, or perhaps it was his gentle, resilient nature that allowed him to navigate the home's complexities with a quiet strength. He seemed to carry a sense of peace within him, even when surrounded by the echoes of our family's past turmoil. As he grew, that peace turned into a profound faith, which became the cornerstone of his life. Growing up without a clear sense of direction, Kurtis could have easily spent his life in our hometown, working a steady job for the City of Garland, and staying tethered to our past. But God had other plans.

Christ called him, and Kurtis answered with faith and courage. He enrolled at the Jackson College of Ministries in Jackson, Mississippi, where his purpose began to crystallize. There, he met his future wife, Carla, and together they envisioned a life of service. After graduating, they married and embarked on a bold mission, serving in the Philippines. It was there that Kurtis' passion for outreach deepened, shaping his calling. Upon returning to the United States, he planted a church in Nashville, where, for the past twenty-eight years, he and Carla have faithfully pastored a growing congregation. Their daughter, Caitlin Dykes, and son-in-law, Travis, are deeply involved in the music ministry, carrying forward the family's legacy of faith and service.

Kurtis didn't just survive the remnants of our broken home—he thrived, becoming a beacon of hope and stability. His calling to the ministry felt almost inevitable as if he was destined to be a vessel of God's grace from the very beginning. I love my brother Kurtis, and I always will. His faith, resilience, and devotion to his calling continue to inspire me.

Conclusion

Reflecting on the lives of my sisters—Carol, Cynthia, and

Charlotte—I'm struck by the profound sadness of what was lost in our childhoods. The innocence, the stability, the sense of security—all were casualties of our parents' dysfunction. Each of my sisters, in their own way, bore the brunt of that loss, their lives marked by the struggle to find what was taken from them.

In sharing these stories, my intention is not to judge, but to offer a glimpse into the complex web of experiences that shaped each of us. Our lives, marked by both sorrow and resilience, are interwoven in ways that only those who shared our journey can fully understand. My hope is that by telling these stories, I can honor my sisters' lives and the strength we all found amidst the challenges of our upbringing.

Carol's journey was one of outward rebellion and inward turmoil, her anger a constant companion. Despite her academic and professional achievements, the shadows of her past loomed large, affecting her relationships and her sense of self-worth. The bright-eyed girl who once had everything she desired was replaced by a woman whose life was a series of battles, both won and lost. Jane's poem, "Daughters of the Bottle," speaks to the hidden struggles of children of alcoholics—those who present a facade of competence and control while silently bearing the weight of their emotional scars. Carol embodied this concept of "competent imposters," appearing outwardly in control but inwardly seething with unresolved anger and pain. Her repeated marriages and public sparring with Mom underscore the internal battles she faced daily, masked by a veneer of control and capability. Despite her outward confidence, success as a teacher, and charm, Carol's life was marked by the turmoil she could never fully escape, reflecting the hidden anguish that Jane's poem so poignantly captures.

Cynthia, on the other hand, internalized her pain. Her quiet demeanor masked a depth of emotion that found expression in her love for music and her fierce independence. Her struggles with relationships, her late-life fight with cancer, and her ultimate grace in facing death speak to a resilience that is both heartbreaking and inspiring. Cynthia embodied the "stay away smiles" mentioned in Jane's poem, presenting a calm and composed exterior while concealing the deep emotional turmoil within. Her quiet demeanor and ability to mask her inner struggles with charm and falsehoods made her seem distant and reserved. The facade of competence and independence she maintained, despite her internal battles and the chaos she experienced, perfectly captures the essence of the stay-away smiles that children of alcoholics often adopt as a shield against the world.

In my view, Charlotte was the most promising of us all, but she faced unimaginable trauma and betrayal. Her spirit was chipped away by the very people who were supposed to protect her. Yet, she found a way to reclaim her life, to rise from the ashes of her past with a newfound strength and independence. Charlotte embodies the lines from Jane's poem, "leaders in their work" and "children of alcoholics always do," as she, like many children of alcoholics, managed to build a stable career while struggling privately with the deep wounds of her upbringing. Her journey reflects the resilience and determination that so often define those who have grown up in chaos—finding a way to lead a fulfilling life, even as they carry the weight of their past.

Their stories are a testament to the enduring impact of our childhood. The dysfunction we grew up in left its mark on all of us, shaping our paths in ways that we continue to understand and come to terms with. As I look back, I see not just the pain and the loss, but also the strength and the resilience that have defined our lives. Carol, Cynthia, and Charlotte's journeys are a part of my own; their struggles and triumphs a reflection of the complex tapestry of our shared history.

The lessons learned from our tumultuous upbringing are both simple and profound. They teach us the value of empathy, the importance of forgiveness, and the necessity of finding our own paths to healing. Each of my sisters navigated their journey in their own unique way, facing down demons that were birthed in our chaotic household.

From Carol, I learned the price of unresolved anger and the importance of seeking peace within oneself. From Cynthia, I learned the power of quiet strength and the grace that can be found even in the face of life's greatest challenges. And from Charlotte, I learned the resilience of the human spirit and how one can rise from the ashes of trauma and forge a new life with independence and dignity.

Our past, marred by the shadows of addiction and dysfunction, shaped us in ways we could never escape. Yet, it also gave us a unique resilience and an ability to find light in the darkest of places. As I reflect on my sisters' lives and the paths we have walked, I am filled with a deep sense of both sorrow and gratitude. Sorrow for the childhood that was lost and gratitude for the strength we found in its wake.

Every time I hear the Beatles, I will think of Cynthia, her passion for music a reminder of the joy that can be found even in the midst of pain. Every time I see a classroom, I will think of Carol, her dedication to her students a testament to her determination to make a difference despite her own struggles. And every time I see a woman who has found her own way after years of co-dependency, I will think of Charlotte, her journey to independence a beacon of hope.

In the end, the greatest lesson we can take from our past is the understanding that healing is a lifelong journey. It requires patience, compassion, and the willingness to confront the shadows of our past. My sisters and I have walked this path in our own ways, and our stories are intertwined with both the pain of our upbringing and the resilience we found within ourselves.

As I look back on our lives, I see a tapestry woven with threads of sorrow and strength, a testament to the enduring power of the human spirit. And in that tapestry, I find the courage to continue my own journey, to seek healing, and to honor the shared memory of my sisters' experiences by living a life filled with empathy, forgiveness, and love.

CHAPTER 17

Postcards from the Journey

Paths in Nature

In 1993, we gathered the Ketchum Chicago team for a transformative Outward Bound weekend at Devil's Lake near Madison, Wisconsin. The beauty of the state park, with its opportunities to hike, rappel, and rock climb, created a deep connection to the natural world. Being in such an awe-inspiring place brought a sense of peace and renewal. In these moments, surrounded by the raw beauty of nature, I feel closest to God, witnessing firsthand the wonders of His creation.

After meeting the physical and mental challenges of the weekend and bonding with our colleagues, the guides directed us to spend an afternoon alone in nature—meditating and journaling. It was an emotionally charged time. As I reflected on the tumultuous years and the personal battles I had faced, I found comfort in the words of Psalm 114: 7-8: *"Tremble, O earth, at the presence of the Lord, at the presence of the God of Jacob, who turned the rock into a pool, the hard rock into springs of water."*

These verses reminded me of the transformative power of faith and resilience. Just as God turned the rock into a pool and the hard rock into springs of water, there was hope that even the hardest moments of my life could be transformed into something life-giving and sustaining. The experiences at Devil's Lake not only fostered my appreciation for nature but also mirrored the internal journey I was on. Each climb, each rappel, was a testament to resilience and faith, reminding me that with determination and trust, even the hardest rock could be transformed into springs of water.

Through the years, I've continued taking photos of paths in nature as we hike in forest preserves and national parks and along mountain trails—from Kane and DuPage counties in Illinois to Starved Rock State Park in Oglesby, Illinois, to Phoenix, Scottsdale, and Sedona, Arizona, to Bend and Crater Lake, Oregon, to Palm Desert and Joshua Tree, California, and to the Black Hills and Badlands of South Dakota. I love the serenity, majesty, and purity of nature, and see God's hand at work when we're out hiking in the places we love.

Paths are a metaphor for expressing the direction of our lives, our journey toward discovering who we're becoming—spiritually, intellectually, and artistically, and in our many life roles. They remind us that if you want real answers and to discover what looms over the horizon, you've got to go the distance. Though painful at times, they tell us the biggest thing about moving forward is looking back at the trail we've journeyed so that we remember the struggles we've endured, how we overcame real challenges, and to illuminate the blazes and signs on the path that will return us safely to where we began.

Sometimes there is no path. What then? In my office is wall art that reminds me of the journey I've been on for so long: *"Do not follow where the path may lead. Go instead where there is no path and leave a trail."*

Find your path or create a new trail!

Historical Pathways

> Copthorne Hotel, Anzac Avenue, Auckland, New Zealand—January 2003
>
> *I'm writing this diary entry in Room 308 at the Copthorne Hotel. The Eckerd College students, their winter term course advisor, Dr. Peter Hammerschmidt, and the business leaders I'm joining have arrived for the America's Cup. Everyone looks relieved to be here.*

On cue, I assume the role I've learned: *Here is a mask. I hide my true self behind the mask.* The serious, orderly side of me often controls my greater need to know, grow, and explore. As we prepare for a month-long adventure on the North and South Islands of New Zealand, I feel that I'm on the precipice of a new discovery.

New pathways beckon: a climb of Dimrill Dale and Moria, traversing the Franz Josef Glacier, and completing the spectacularly scenic, thirty-mile Milford Track. These are more than physical challenges; they symbolize my internal journey. I feel a new spiritual longing for closeness with the Infinite Wisdom of my Creator and the internal peace and calm that I must know. The Universe calls for my discovery of who I am, what I am to do, and what I am to become.

Peter's words to our group echo in my head: *"The independence of character empowers us to act rather than to be acted upon."* His message is a call to embrace our true selves, to act with intention and purpose, and to shed the masks that hide our authenticity.

Each step taken on these paths brings me closer to my Creator, guiding me toward the peace and calm I yearn for. The path ahead is uncertain but full of promise. It is a journey not just through the breathtaking landscapes of New Zealand, but through the depths of my own soul. Here, I hope to find the courage to remove my mask and embrace the person I'm meant to be.

CLAUDE MONET'S HOME, GIVERNY, FRANCE–OCTOBER 2005

I return to Claude Monet's home for another weekend visit while traveling in France. The weather is a beautiful sixty-five degrees. The garden is bathed in rich sunlight. Footsteps are heard on the gravel walkways as people pass, speaking in French and German and enjoying their families on a glorious Sunday afternoon. I love France. I love this place. I've been here many times over the past decade.

Monet, the renowned French Impressionist painter, had a deep affection for his garden at Giverny, which he famously said was his "most beautiful masterpiece." Monet's Garden was not only a source of personal joy but also an inspiration for many of his greatest works. He once said, "I perhaps owe having become a painter to flowers," underscoring his lifelong fascination with nature and the central role his garden played in his artistic vision.

As I wander through the serene beauty of Monet's Garden, I'm struck by how this place remains unchanged—enduring, peaceful, and true. The vibrant colors of the flowers, the tranquil lily pond, and the timeless paintings of haystacks he captured from fields nearby evoke a sense of stability and calm that contrasts sharply with the inner turmoil I often feel. Here, surrounded by such beauty, I'm reminded of the simplicity and purity of nature, which stands in stark contrast to the complexity and chaos of my thoughts.

In these moments, the words from Ralph Vaughan Williams' "The Lark Ascending" come to mind, echoing the profound connection between nature and the divine:

He rises and begins to round,
He drops the silver chain of sound,

Of many links without a break, In chirrup,
whistle, slur and shake...

These lines, filled with the imagery of a lark's ascent, remind me of
the ethereal presence of God in the beauty around me. The patterns
of sunlight and shadows, always changing, conjure a sense of God's
artistry in nature. The lark's song, like a silver chain of sound, feels like
a direct link to the divine, calling me to rise above my earthly concerns.

As I continue walking through the garden, I feel the weight of my
worries lifting slightly. The next lines of the poem play in my mind,
offering further solace:

For singing till his heaven fills,
'Tis love of earth that he instils,
And ever winging up and up,
Our valley is his golden cup,
And he the wine which overflows
To lift us with him as he goes...

The lark's continuous ascent, instilling a love of earth, mirrors my own
longing for a deeper connection with the world around me. As I reflect
on my life and purpose, I realize how these worries about time, worth,
and significance weigh heavily on my spirit. Questions of whether I'm
making a difference or if I truly matter had created a blockage within
me, constricting my energy and clouding my spirit.

In this reflective state, I turn to prayer, seeking guidance and purpose.
"God, I pray, guide me in my life..." The beauty and tranquility of Monet's
home and garden offered a perfect backdrop for such introspection.
Here, away from the daily grind, I felt a renewed sense of possibility
and hope.

As I contemplate the enduring qualities of Monet's Garden, my journey comes into greater focus. Like the haystacks in Monet's paintings, I search for the way forward, looking for signs of stability and purpose amidst the shifting landscapes of my life. The final lines of the poem encapsulate this feeling of transcendence and the ongoing search for meaning:

> *Till lost on his aërial rings In light,*
> *and then the fancy sings.*

The lark's flight, ascending higher and higher until lost in the light, symbolizes my own aspiration to rise above the chaos and find clarity. It reminds me that life's journey, with its patterns of light and shadow, is a continuous process of seeking and finding, of rising and being lifted by the divine presence in the natural world around us.

Spiritual Pathways

CHARTRES CATHEDRAL, FRANCE—JUNE 2007

I remember the first time I saw the Chartres Cathedral. I was traveling from Paris by car. As we topped a hill, this majestic church climbed out of rolling wheat fields in the countryside of France. When Chartres Cathedral was built in the thirteenth century, a medieval labyrinth was set into the floor of the church. Since most people could never make it to Jerusalem, the heart of Christendom, they would go instead to churches in Canterbury, Santiago de Compostela, and Chartres. Once there, the faithful would end their pilgrimage by walking the forty-foot-wide labyrinth to the center. Then, they would slowly retrace their steps to regain the "outside world." The path of the labyrinth symbolizes the journey of human life leading to ultimate victory over Evil through Jesus Christ —the journey to truth.

The cathedral's architecture is a testament to human devotion and the spirit to serve God, manifesting in its grandeur and intricate details. Among the most captivating features are the stained glass windows, especially those positioned lower in the structure. These windows were created by the tradesmen of Chartres to advertise their craft and subtly protest the taxation imposed by the clergy. Each pane of glass tells a story not only of biblical scenes but also of the everyday lives and struggles of the people who built this incredible monument to faith. The trade windows of Chartres, as detailed in Philip Ball's *Universe of Stone: A Biography of Chartres Cathedral*, highlight the intricate relationship between the cathedral and the various guilds and tradespeople of the medieval period. They depict scenes that not only highlight biblical stories but also illustrate the daily lives and work of the tradespeople who sponsored them.

These stained glass windows reflect a profound sense of community and humanity's collaboration to serve a higher purpose. They capture the essence of our connection to the divine, illustrating both reverence for God and resilience of spirit. Through their art, tradesmen communicated devotion and dissent, leaving a legacy that speaks to the enduring bond between faith and daily life. This fusion of religious and social history makes the windows of Chartres a testament to the unity and spirit of its people.

I'm always drawn to Chartres Cathedral by God's presence in this incredible place. Each visit feels like a pilgrimage, a journey into the heart of my faith. The light filtering through the stained glass creates a kaleidoscope of colors on the stone floor, reminding me of the divine light that guides us through our darkest hours. The beauty and simplicity of the cathedral, both in its grand design and its intricate details, reflect the glory of God and the dedication of those who built it.

Walking the labyrinth, I'm reminded of the countless faithful who have traversed this path before me. Over hundreds of years, their feet have worn the stone smooth, leaving a tangible mark of their devotion.

The floor, polished by the passage of so many pilgrims, tells a story of unending faith and perseverance. Each step I take feels connected to the millions who have sought peace, guidance, and a closer connection to God within these walls. The labyrinth is not just a symbol; it is a living testament to the enduring spirit of humanity's quest for the divine.

In these moments, the words from Psalm 24:7-10, echo in my mind, infusing the experience with a sense of divine grandeur:

> *Lift up your heads, O gates!*
> *And be lifted up, O ancient doors,*
> *that the King of glory may come in.*
> *Who is this King of glory?*
> *The Lord, strong and mighty,*
> *the Lord, mighty in battle!*
> *Lift up your heads, O gates!*
> *And lift them up, O ancient doors,*
> *that the King of glory may come in.*
> *Who is this King of glory?*
> *The Lord of hosts, he is the King of glory!*

These verses resonate with the sacred atmosphere of Chartres, reminding me of the divine presence that has been welcomed here for centuries. The cathedral's gates and doors, standing tall and ancient, have indeed lifted up to let in the King of Glory, reflecting the enduring faith and devotion of those who have worshipped here.

Outside, the courtyard of Chartres Cathedral is graced by the presence of stately linden trees, standing in quiet testament to the passage of time. These trees, with their symmetrical shape and dense foliage, create a serene and contemplative environment. They've been pruned into neat, straight lines, reflecting the order and precision that echoes the divine harmony found within the cathedral. The linden trees, often used in European formal gardens and courtyards, symbolize strength and resilience. Their roots dig deep into the earth, anchoring them firmly, much like the unwavering faith of the pilgrims who have come here through the centuries.

The linden trees whisper of the countless souls who have paused beneath their branches, seeking shade and solace, reflecting on their own spiritual journeys. They stand as silent witnesses to the devotion and prayers that have been offered here, their leaves rustling gently in the breeze as if in quiet reverence to the divine.

These visits to Chartres Cathedral remind me of the ongoing journey of my own faith. Just as the labyrinth symbolizes the winding path of human life, filled with twists and turns, my visits here are moments of clarity, each one capturing a fleeting glimpse of truth. They remind me that my journey is ongoing and that each day is an opportunity to align my life more closely with the reflections of my heart. In this pursuit, I find a new pathway to truth, one that is guided by love, purpose, and the enduring beauty of the present moment.

The stained glass windows, with their stories of craftsmanship and protest, and the linden trees, with their steadfast presence, reflect the timeless spirit of man to serve God. They stand as a testament to the countless souls who have walked these halls, seeking peace, inspiration and a deeper connection to the divine. Through hundreds of years, the cathedral has been a beacon of faith, a place where the spirit of God and the spirit of man meet in a harmonious blend of art and devotion.

In these hallowed halls, I'm reminded that the journey to truth is not a solitary one. It's a path walked by many before me, and it will be walked by many after. The cathedral, with its labyrinth, stained glass, towering spires, and steadfast presence, symbolizes the enduring quest for understanding, faith, and the eternal light of God's love. Each visit renews my spirit and reaffirms my commitment to live a life guided by the divine truths reflected in this sacred space.

THE MERCHANT HOTEL, BELFAST, IRELAND—JUNE 2011

Walking through Pottinger's Entry on a visit to Northern Ireland, I'm struck by the historical weight of this arched passageway. It knifes into the one-time waterfront streets of Belfast, snaking between warehouse blocks and leading down to the quayside that was destroyed by a German aerial assault in World War II. This gateway, named after the prominent Pottinger family—a lineage notable for their contributions to commerce and politics in Belfast—has connected multiple gener-ations to the world of commerce, social trends, lifestyle interests, and sources of knowledge that fueled their lives.

Pottinger's Entry, with its narrow alleyways dating back to the 1600s, serves as a powerful allegory for my own journey and the pursuit of purpose. Just as this historic portal opens up to broader opportunities and connections, discovering the right path to the hearts and minds of others—and to my own heart—can transform lives. It reminds me that true fulfillment and profound personal growth are attainable when we navigate life's labyrinth with courage and faith. The ancient cobblestones of Pottinger's Entry whisper stories of resilience and discovery, echoing my own quest for meaning and connection in a world full of hidden wonders.

In this reflective state, I turn to prayer, seeking guidance and purpose. I remember Psalm 81:7: *"In your distress you called and I rescued you, I answered you out of a thundercloud; I tested you at the waters of Meribah."* I consider how much my mental and physical state is affected by my frustrations and worries. Here, away from the daily grind, I feel a renewed sense of possibility and hope. I realize that living in the quality of this moment requires a shift in perspective. It means embracing each day with purpose, seeking out the beauty and truth in every experience, and letting go of what is fleeting. It means allowing my heart to guide my actions, reflecting the love and kindness I wish to see in the world.

Belfast's history is deeply intertwined with its tumultuous past, especially during the period known as the Troubles. For generations, the British and the people of Northern Ireland have struggled and fought, their history marked by this conflict that deeply scarred the city and its inhabitants. The Troubles, a violent conflict from the late 1960s to 1998, saw intense strife between unionists, who were mainly Protestant and wanted Northern Ireland to remain part of the United Kingdom, and nationalists, who were mostly Catholic and sought reunification with the Republic of Ireland. This period left profound marks on the city, both physically and emotionally.

Walking through neighborhoods like Falls Road and Shankill Road, I feel the weight of this history and the echoes of conflict. The murals on the walls tell stories of resistance, hope, and the quest for peace. The peace lines, still standing, are poignant reminders of division but also of the ongoing journey toward healing and unity.

As I walk, I find myself reflecting on my own past, the memories tumbling back to me. It's difficult to put into words what I felt as a boy, living in a mystery world filled with constant fear. I felt fragile and divided. Deep inside, the fear and vagueness were ugly and formless, making them hard to uncover.

Fear and anger found a cruel intersection, terrorizing my mind. I could never imagine the mistreatment, cruel and so very complete, that my mother endured and that I witnessed. It was always frightening. I never should have been made to cower in my own home by my own father.

The lies. If I was told once, I was told lies thousands of times to console me, to turn back my anger and disappointment, to win my affection. And without even a hint of remorse, a promise made was again a promise broken. I'm sure I must've cried, felt sad and disappointed. But I buried these feelings and went forward—again and again and again.

As I walk these streets, my life feels like the walls of the Grand Canyon: at the surface, it is flat and does not evoke emotion. As I endeavor to cut away the surface, buried down below is a beauty that is majestic and powerful and inspiring in its simplicity. When will the beauty shine forth?

We all die a little every day. Something is taken. I don't slow down or even for a moment consider what it meant, why it happened, why I experienced it, and how it changed me. A still life in clichés, dismissing the power and the significance of the moment. What is it when you wish to be in touch with the soul, to know who, and why, and what really matters?

As I walk down Falls Road and Shankill Road, I feel the presence of those who have endured, who have fought their battles, and still found the strength to seek peace. Their resilience mirrors my own journey. The scars of conflict are visible, yet so is the determination to heal, to move forward, to create a future defined by harmony rather than discord. It is a testament to the strength of the human spirit and the capacity for renewal.

I stand in the Titanic Quarter, once the bustling shipyards where the RMS *Titanic* and her sister ships, the *Olympic* and *Britannic*, were built. Now, it is a vibrant area celebrating this legacy. The Harland and Wolff shipyard, where these magnificent vessels were constructed, serves as a reminder of the city's industrial prowess and the ingenuity of its people. The Titanic Belfast Museum, situated here, offers a deep dive into the history of the ill-fated ship and the lives of those who built her.

I can come to terms with a past that has imprisoned me. I don't want to live this way anymore. Walking through the shipyards and reflecting on the lives of those who built these great ships, I realize that I, too, can build something enduring from the pain and experiences of my past. I can transform my life just as these shipbuilders transformed steel into magnificent vessels.

The city's spirit of resilience is also evident in its tumultuous history of conflict and reconciliation. These communities, with their modest brick homes and vibrant gardens, reflect a resilience that is both humbling and inspiring. Despite the scars of the past, there is a palpable sense of determination to move forward, to create a future defined by harmony rather than discord. It is a testament to the strength of the human spirit and the capacity for renewal.

I stop and pray:

> God, I pray You will refine me as silver is refined, test me as gold is tested. Just as the Israelites were tested in the wilderness, You have shown me that life is a laboratory of faith. I have seen Your incredible power and grace in my life, through moments of joy and moments of pain. Yet, like others, I have sometimes faltered, grumbling and complaining instead of trusting in Your provision. Teach me to trust in Your ability to provide, even when the path ahead seems uncertain.
>
> Refine me, Lord, through the trials I face. Help me to understand that You are strengthening my faith and confirming the sincerity of my commitment to you. I know You do not tempt me, for temptation comes from the enemy. Instead, You use these challenges to purify my heart and draw me closer to You.
>
> In my darkest hours, when I am tested by fear and doubt, remind me of Your promises. Just as gold is refined in the fire, let the trials I face strip away my impurities, leaving a heart that is pure and steadfast in faith. Help me to see that these tests are not punishments but opportunities to grow stronger in my walk with You.
>
> May I emerge from these tests with a faith that is resilient and unshakeable, reflecting Your glory and grace. Refine me,

Lord, so that I may shine brightly for You, a testament to Your
unfailing love and faithfulness. In Jesus' name, I pray. Amen.

In these moments of reflection and discovery, I feel connected to
the enduring spirit of Belfast, much like I do in the sacred spaces of
Chartres Cathedral. Both places, though vastly different, remind me of
the resilience and faith that define the human experience. They inspire
me to continue my journey with a renewed sense of purpose and hope,
seeking the divine in the every day and finding strength in the stories
of those who have walked these paths before me.

CHAPTER 18

The Ripple Effect

A week after Sue's heart attack in December 2022, I was walking our dogs on a prairie path in Geneva when I felt the symptoms of a panic attack creeping up on me. I had barely slept over the preceding days because Sue had been in Delnor Northwestern Hospital, recovering from the procedures to place stents in her coronary arteries. I was driving back and forth from home to Delnor multiple times every day, keeping our family and friends updated on Sue's condition, caring for our dogs, and consulting with two clients. One day, a little voice in my head whispered, "You're getting sick," and I did.

While on that walk, I was talking on my mobile when I hit a patch of black ice on the asphalt path and went down hard on my left hand and wrist, fracturing it. The broken bone compounded my feelings of anxiety.

The irony was glaring: While Sue was fine and recovering from her life-threatening ordeal, I was falling apart. The ringing in my ears was relentless. I was dizzy. My blood pressure spiked to 160 over 90, and I literally could not sleep. It got so bad that I thought I might be destined for the hospital myself.

One Sunday morning, lying in bed awake at 3:30 a.m., I felt a sharp pain between my shoulder blades and the thud of my heartbeat in my ears. Desperation clawed at me. I finally got out of bed and announced I was going to the ER.

At the Delnor Emergency Room, they performed an EKG to check the electrical activity of my heart and blood tests to look for markers of heart damage, such as troponin levels. They also conducted a chest X-ray to rule out any structural issues and a series of blood pressure readings. I sat in the waiting area for two hours, from 4:00 a.m. until 6:00 a.m., as a parade of new patients arrived and checked in for treatment. The ER medical team repeated the tests and announced that my heart was fine. The relief was momentary. A few days later, my doctor suggested I find counseling and helped identify a psychologist specializing in panic disorders and PTSD.

The despair I felt during this time was overwhelming. The constant fear of my own health collapsing, combined with the stress of Sue's recovery, created a relentless cycle of anxiety. I was haunted by the thought that I was not strong enough to support her, that my own body and mind were betraying me when I needed to be at my best. This period stripped me of the illusion of control, exposing the raw vulnerability beneath. Seeking help was a step toward reclaiming my life, but it was also an admission of my fragility. It was a humbling realization that even the strongest hearts can falter and that asking for help is not a sign of weakness but of courage and self-preservation.

I met Scott Gleeson, a Christ-centered counselor specializing in treating trauma, PTSD, depression, and relationship issues, and he agreed to take me as a new patient. Over the next year, Scott established a trusting relationship by actively listening to me. He showed genuine empathy and compassion for my life experiences and put together a thoughtful treatment plan. He encouraged self-reflection and guided me through Robert Jackman's *Healing Your Lost Inner Child*, a profound journey of reconnecting with and healing from past traumas.

Through our sessions together and on my own as I read Jackman's book, I began to strip away the pain I had carried for a lifetime, like peeling away heavy coats of paint. One by one, I removed these layers. The first was the "coating" from my early childhood. As I revisited those memories, I felt a sense of healing as the light of honesty shined in. It felt good to finally see myself clearly. I realized I was a good kid, frightened and confused about my chaotic world. Understanding that I couldn't change things back then brought profound relief and self-compassion.

I couldn't imagine any other human being experiencing what I did growing up. The constant chaos, the unpredictability of living with an alcoholic parent, the emotional neglect, the fear of emotional and physical violence—it all seemed like a unique form of torture. One day during a session, Scott looked at me with deep compassion and said, "You do realize that had you been living here, in Illinois, child protective services would have been called in, and you would have been taken from your family." His words pierced through the fog of my pain, bringing a profound realization of the gravity of my past.

That revelation hit hard. It was a validation of the severity of my childhood experiences and an acknowledgment of the resilience it took to survive them. Understanding this, I began to see my past not just as a series of unfortunate events but as a testament to my strength and endurance. It was a profound shift in perspective that allowed me to start forgiving myself for the vulnerabilities I had always seen as weaknesses.

My journey through therapy was about understanding my past and reclaiming my life. It was about breaking the cycle of despair and finding a path to genuine healing. Each session with Scott was a step toward stripping away the layers of pain to reveal a core of resilience and hope. I came to realize that my vulnerabilities were not flaws but scars of battles fought and survived. They were marks of my humanity, symbols of my journey from darkness to light.

In reflecting on these experiences, I'm reminded of the ripple effect of our actions and choices. Every step we take and every decision we make has the potential to influence not just our lives but the lives of those around us and the generations that follow. The process of healing and self-discovery is ongoing, but it starts with acknowledging our pain and seeking help.

Understanding the deep impact of this journey, I committed to meeting with my siblings and my own children to share what I had learned about myself and to let them finally come to know the real me after a lifetime. It was essential for me to connect with them on a deeper level, to offer them the authenticity and vulnerability that had been missing for so long. By doing so, I hoped to foster stronger relationships and break the cycle of silence and misunderstanding that had plagued our family.

Jackman's powerful words from his book *Healing Your Lost Inner Child* resonate deeply with me: *"Our pain is looking for acknowledgment. Once we connect to our wounding, a doorway for healing opens."* This quote encapsulates my journey and the hope that by acknowledging our pain and sharing our truths, we can open the door to healing and create ripples of positive change that will extend far beyond our immediate reach.

As this chapter draws to a close, I want to take a moment to acknowledge you, my readers. I know that many of you have walked similar paths, burdened by struggles, grief, and pain that at times may have seemed insurmountable. Whether you have faced these challenges in silence, or alongside others, your journey is a testament to your resilience and strength. I honor the work you have done, often in the quiet spaces of your heart, to heal and to seek a brighter, more authentic life.

I recognize the deep longing for healing and recovery that lives within us all, the desire to find peace amidst the chaos of our pasts. Your commitment to this journey—whether whispered in the dark or shouted from the rooftops—is a courageous act of self-love and transformation. It is through these shared experiences, these moments of raw honesty and brave vulnerability, that we find the power to heal, not just ourselves but those around us.

As you continue on your own path, remember that each step forward, no matter how small, is a victory. Every moment of acknowledgment, every instance of facing your pain head-on, opens the door wider for healing and renewal. Your efforts, your courage, and your willingness to embrace the truth are the seeds of change that will grow and flourish, touching lives in ways you may never fully know.

This chapter marks a turning point not just in my life, but in our shared journey toward healing. It is a testament to the power of vulnerability, to the courage it takes to face our deepest fears, and to the strength we find in acknowledging our pain. As I move forward, I do so with the knowledge that every ripple of healing and honesty has the potential to transform not just my life, but the lives of those I hold dear—and the lives of those who read these words.

CHAPTER 19

Embracing the Light

Forty years after my original visit, I returned to Big Springs Cemetery to rediscover Vivian Morgan's gravesite. It was January 2024, and a cold wind was blowing, nipping at my ears and cheeks. The cemetery was silent, with only the soft rustling of grass among the headstones to break the stillness. As I stood there, I couldn't help but feel the sting once more—the revelation from years earlier that my DNA test had proven he was not, as I had once believed, my grandfather. The sun tried to pierce through the cloud cover, forming a faint halo that did little to warm the chill air around me. Leaves cartwheeled across the gravesites, adding a fleeting sense of movement to the somber scene.

I walked among the headstones for an hour, nearly giving up hope. Just as I was ready to leave, an inner voice urged me to check near the entry gate by the elders. There, at last, I found his grave. Sue joined me, and together we stood in silence. Tears flowed as I began to contemplate the long journey to uncover the truth.

My maternal grandmother, Gladys Morgan, had an affair outside her marriage that led to my mother's birth. Over the years, it became clear that my mother, in turn, conceived my sister Carol under similar circumstances. Carol's own choices later resulted in the birth of my

158 SHADOWS OF SOBRIETY

brother, Kurtis. These intertwined events—across generations—have profoundly shaped the trajectory of our family's story.

Dad made choices, too—choices that led to his alcoholism and created a turbulent home environment where love and pain were often indistinguishable. His decision to drink wasn't just about alcohol; it was about embracing recklessness. This choice cast a long shadow over our family, leaving us with scars that would take a lifetime to heal. Yet, despite his flaws, there was something redeeming in his behavior. He didn't abandon Mom when he found out about her infidelity. He believed in the sanctity of marriage and stayed committed to it, even while violating those very values through his own infidelity.

Alcohol seemed to act as both a veil and a catalyst for Dad's decisions, blurring the lines between integrity and its absence. His choices often reflected a man wrestling with his own moral compass. One stark example was his reckless involvement with Red Bankston in the kidnapping of Red's uncle—a decision that showcased a blatant disregard for both integrity and the law. It was as though alcohol fueled his ability to rationalize such behavior, allowing him to bypass the internal voice that might have otherwise held him back.

And then there was the night Dad stole the safe from the supermarket. Whether it was desperation, a misguided attempt to fix what had already unraveled, or the influence of alcohol clouding his judgment, we'll never know. But that choice had consequences that rippled through our lives. It became another chapter in the story of a man whose decisions often betrayed his better nature. The theft wasn't just about the money; it symbolized how far things had fallen for him, and for all of us.

Yet, there were moments that revealed the core of his character, even through the haze of alcohol. After Unk's death, when Dad discovered $18,000 in cash hidden in his home, he faced a pivotal decision. In a world where alcohol often muddied his judgment, this act of honesty stood out. Instead of pocketing the money, Dad chose to give it to

Mimmie, Unk's sister. It was a moment where his integrity surfaced—perhaps briefly fighting against the pull of his darker impulses.

Alcohol may have moderated his actions, but it did not completely erase his sense of right and wrong. His internal conflict, visible in decisions like these, revealed a man caught between the influence of alcohol and his inherent, though often compromised, moral compass.

My feelings toward my parents have evolved. I don't hate them, and I don't love them either. Today, I better understand and accept who they were. They had their struggles, and their actions were influenced by battles I may never fully comprehend. They did the best they could with the tools they had, even if it fell short of what I needed. Recognizing their humanity and flaws, I've found peace and acceptance, knowing their journey shaped mine in ways that have led me to understanding.

This realization is part of the broader irony of my life: By day, I was a polished public relations executive, crafting narratives and managing perceptions to ensure everything appeared perfect on the surface. Yet, by night, I was grappling with my own demons, trying to keep the chaos of my personal life hidden from view. This dual existence created a constant tug-of-war, highlighting the stark disparity between my outward success and inner turmoil. It felt as if I was living two lives, each demanding a different version of myself, leaving me exhausted and fragmented. This duality underscores a universal truth: No matter how put-together someone may appear, they can still be fighting profound personal battles. My journey is a testament to the power of resilience and the importance of confronting inner turmoil.

Reflecting on my life, I'm reminded of Matthew Perry's words. "You have to have all of your dreams come true to realize they are the wrong dreams." This sentiment resonates deeply, highlighting how my expectations and dreams evolved in light of truth and understanding.

I once had the honor of being onstage at the historic Red House Theater in Taipei, Taiwan. The crowd below, mesmerized by the actors, reminded me of the stages of my life, where each actor left indelible marks on who I've become. My journey has unfolded across diverse and vivid scenes, each a distinct chapter in my story.

The Big Empty, with its vast open spaces and quiet solitude, instilled in me resilience and introspection. My grandfather, John Henry Burton, left a legacy that echoed across the prairie, shaping the very fabric of my being. Garland, with its blend of innocence and turmoil, deeply influenced my foundational years. In Cleburne, a smaller town, I discovered the profound effect a family's legacy has on a community through generations, along with the value of simplicity and the strength of community, which fostered personal growth.

Naperville offered stability and a canvas for my ambitions. Nature's trails provided solace, helping me reconnect with myself amid chaos. Chartres Cathedral, with its sacred halls and stained glass, reminded me of my spiritual journey. Monet's Garden, full of ethereal beauty, symbolized artistic inspiration and wonder. Climbing Mount Kilimanjaro taught me perseverance and the joy of reaching new heights. Belfast's rich history and resilient spirit deepened my appreciation for strength and determination.

Every place has shaped who I am today. Each stage, rich with memories, taught me resilience, growth, and acceptance. They've led me to a profound understanding of my journey, where every experience and lesson is part of my intricate and beautiful life.

Life is about choices. Some bring joy, others sorrow, but all are part of our journey. My life has been shaped by the choices of those before me, and I've made my own in response to their legacy. I chose to confront my past, seek understanding and healing, and break the cycle of dysfunction that plagued my family for generations.

Returning to Big Springs Cemetery was a choice driven by the need for closure and to honor those who came before me. Standing there with Sue, I realized the journey to truth is not just about uncovering the past but making choices that lead to a better future.

We all have the power to make choices that define our lives. Gladys, my mother, Carol, and my father each made choices that set the course for their lives and their children's lives. I chose to return to this cemetery, face the past, and find peace in the truth.

As I stood by Vivian Morgan's grave, I felt a sense of resolve. The choices of the past may have shaped me, but they don't define me. As Bill Wrigley, Jr., my client and heir to the Wrigley chewing gum fortune, once said, "Our legacy is not the past. Our legacy will be the future we create for ourselves and for others."

I have the power to make my own choices, forge my path, and create a legacy of healing and hope for future generations. Life is about choices, and each one is an opportunity to shape our destiny. As Sue and I left the cemetery, I felt a renewed sense of purpose. The journey to truth is ongoing, and with each choice I make, I'm writing my story, one that honors the past but looks forward to a brighter future.

As I stand at the edge of this memoir, looking back over the vast landscape of my journey, I'm filled with reflection and gratitude. The path from the shadows of my childhood to the light of today has been long and arduous, marked by moments of despair but also incredible resilience and growth.

Throughout this journey, I've learned that healing is not a destination but a continuous process. Every day presents new challenges and opportunities for growth. I've come to understand that the pain and struggles of my past don't define me; they've shaped me into the person I am today. I'm stronger, more compassionate, and more attuned to the suffering of others because of the trials I've endured.

Faith has been my guiding star, illuminating the darkest corners of my soul and providing me with the strength to persevere. In the moments when I felt most alone, I turned to God, and He answered. Psalm 81:7 reminds me, *"In your distress you called and I rescued you."* This truth has been my anchor, reminding me that even in the stormiest seas, I'm never truly alone.

Gratitude and forgiveness have been essential companions on this journey. I've learned to forgive those who caused me pain, understanding that holding onto anger and resentment only binds me to the past. Letting go has been a liberating act of self-love. I'm also profoundly grateful for the lessons learned and the strength gained from my experiences. Each scar is a testament to my resilience and a reminder of the battles I've fought and won.

As I look to the future, I'm filled with hope and purpose. I'm committed to using my experiences to help others navigate their own shadows. Whether through sharing my story, offering support, or simply being a beacon of hope, I know my journey has meaning beyond my healing. I aspire to continue growing, seeking purpose, and finding inner peace, knowing the journey itself is a sacred gift.

Reflecting on this journey, I'm reminded of the words of Elaine de Kooning. When asked what it was like to work in the shadow of her famous husband, Willem de Kooning, a renowned abstract expressionist painter, she responded, "I don't paint in his shadow; I paint in his light." These words resonate deeply with me. For so long, I was enveloped by the lingering weight of my past, my pain, and my fears. But now, I see that I am not defined by those lingering specters. Instead, I can choose to live in the light of the lessons learned, the love found, and the faith that has guided me.

To those who have guided my path, encouraged me, and journeyed with me, I offer my heartfelt thanks and honor you:

Lonnie Hitchcock, my kindergarten teacher: Mrs. Hitchcock, with her gentle demeanor and endless patience, was the first to nurture my curiosity and love for learning. Her classroom was a sanctuary where I felt safe and encouraged to explore the world. The friendships I made at Blue Jean Kindergarten have lasted a lifetime. Mrs. Hitchcock always remembered to send newspaper clippings and notes about my progress, which meant the world to me. She taught us the basics of education and imparted the importance of kindness and curiosity. Her belief in my potential planted the seeds for a lifelong love of learning and self-discovery.

Jenny Bisbee, who first taught me to swim: Jenny, with her infectious enthusiasm and supportive nature, turned her pool into a place of joy and accomplishment. She instilled in me not just the ability to swim but also the confidence to tackle challenges head-on. In those waters, I found a sense of freedom and self-assurance that transcended the pool. Her encouragement helped me overcome my fears, and her belief in my abilities taught me the value of perseverance and courage.

Jim Rose, my high school journalism teacher: Mr. Rose, affectionately known as "Teacher," with his unwavering dedication and sharp wit, ignited my passion for storytelling. He taught me the power of words and the importance of integrity in journalism, shaping my future in ways I never imagined. Under his guidance, I learned that journalism was more than reporting facts; it was about uncovering truths and giving voice to the voiceless. His lessons on ethics and narrative craft remain a cornerstone of my professional ethos.

David McHam, my professor of journalism at SMU: Professor McHam guided me through the intricacies of journalism with wisdom and insight. A renowned journalist and First Amendment advocate, he taught writing and communications law at several universities and authored the book *Law and the Media in Texas*. His illustrious career includes being named the outstanding journalism teacher in the nation by the Society of Professional Journalists in 1994. His mentorship, grounded in his extensive experience and education, inspired me to strive for excellence and integrity, emphasizing journalism's noble role in promoting change and justice. His influence has left an indelible mark on my life and career.

Dax Cowart, my inspiration for living life in the face of adversity: Dax, with his remarkable strength and resilience, showed me that even in the darkest times, the human spirit can prevail. His story of perseverance has been a constant source of motivation and courage in my own life. Dax's journey through unimaginable pain and his unwavering resolve to advocate for patient rights taught me the true meaning of courage and determination. His influence reminds me daily that we have the power to rise above our circumstances and impact the world positively.

Stanley Marcus, the merchant prince of Neiman Marcus: "Mr. Stanley," as I and others knew him, was a steadfast advocate for the oppressed and downtrodden. He taught me the importance of standing up for causes that matter, championing minority viewpoints, and amplifying those whose voices must be heard. Despite his wealth and status, he took a genuine interest in my life, using his keen intellect and profound generosity to support my aspirations. His mentorship and advocacy opened doors that significantly shaped my career and personal growth. Through his example, I learned that true success is not only about personal achievements but also about the positive impact we have on others.

Bill Heyman, the real leader behind the careers of every great leader in public relations: Bill, with his profound humility, wisdom, and unwavering loyalty, has been a guiding force in my professional journey. His friendship, belief in my potential, and steadfast support have been the bedrock of my achievements. Bill's mentorship taught me invaluable lessons about listening to others, strategic thinking, ethical practices, and the importance of building meaningful relationships. His example of servant leadership continues to inspire me to lead with integrity and empathy. Bill's influence has not only shaped my career but has also touched my heart, reminding me of the true essence of leadership: to uplift and empower those around you.

Dr. Peter Hammerschmidt has taught me more about leadership through the way he lives his life than anyone else. A paragon of integrity and compassion, Peter embodies true leadership, not just in his words but in his actions. Sensing that I needed to rekindle a spark in my heart and challenge my soul, he invited me into his world of outdoor adventures. Each journey became an opportunity to experience the freedom and wonder of nature, deepening the bond between us. For those shared moments under open skies, I am forever grateful. Peter's teachings and actions have consistently inspired me to lead with empathy and purpose. Even in the face of adversity, I've admired how he lives his life with resilience, humility, and servant leadership. His example has profoundly shaped my own approach to leadership, reminding me of the importance of authenticity and compassion.

Al Golin, whose humanity and pioneering spirit in public relations set a standard of excellence: Al's commitment to ethical communication and his innovative approach have been a guiding light in my career. He understood the power of building a great culture and taking care of people with a "high touch" in the age of "high tech." Al's vision and humanity set a benchmark for excellence in public relations, teaching me the importance of trust, transparency, and human connection in professional practice.

Betsy Plank, the First Lady of Public Relations: Betsy's wisdom and passion left an indelible mark on my professional ethos. In 2006 at the Public Relations Society of America's annual Conference in Salt Lake City, as Conference Chair, I noticed Betsy missing from our pre-dinner meeting. Later, she appeared for dinner, and I asked where she had been. With her characteristic warmth, she touched my arm and said, "I never stay at the conference hotel. I stay with the PRSSA students. I would rather be with them." This simple yet profound choice highlighted her unwavering commitment to the next generation. Betsy co-founded PRSSA and consistently prioritized mentoring students over her own comfort. Her advocacy for education and mentorship inspired my work as chair and a board member of the Plank Center for Leadership in Public Relations. Betsy's legacy of leadership, dedication to education, and commitment to nurturing new talent continue to guide my efforts to foster growth and excellence in the field. Betsy had a signature line for those she loved: "You lit up my sky." In truth, it was *Betsy* who lit up my sky.

Dr. Bruce Berger, a man for all seasons: Bruce's deep understanding of communication has profoundly enriched my knowledge and practice, significantly shaping my approach to strategic communication. He looks into our hearts through the questions he poses, knowing pain and loss and the power of the Living God. His dedication to teaching and research, coupled with his courage and leadership, has significantly influenced my intellectual and professional growth. I'll never forget when Bruce invited me to support Whirlpool's employee communications in Milan, Italy. Bruce always makes time for his mentees and students, embodying the highest standards of mentorship. Beyond his professional insights, Bruce's wisdom and empathy have provided me with greater hope, purpose, and understanding. His scholarship and mentorship have emphasized continuous learning and ethical practice, inspiring me to pursue excellence and compassion in all aspects of my life.

Ron DeFeo, my dearest friend and colleague: Guided by his faith, family, and focus on health, Ron lives by the word "Providential." When confronted with the specter of pancreatic cancer, he surrounded himself with prayer warriors, trusted our Lord, and sought treatment through a world-class medical team in Dallas. He beat cancer, praise God! His faith and encouragement always inspire me to do more in my life. Ron's insightful guidance and strategic acumen have guided his path as Chief Communications Officer at American Airlines. His journey of faith and resilience serves as a powerful testament to the strength of belief and the impact of unwavering support.

Gary Grates, my longtime friend, colleague, and confidant: In a world where authenticity is often overshadowed by superficiality, Gary is a beacon of genuine leadership and unwavering integrity. His enduring loyalty to friends and colleagues is matched only by his boundless spirit for life and his commitment to uplifting the legacy of others. In a profession too often marked by pretenders and self-promotion, Gary exemplifies what it means to lead with authenticity and honor. He possesses an innate ability to seek and follow the truth, guiding others with a wisdom that is both rare and inspiring. His legacy is not just in the accolades he has received, but in the countless lives he has touched with his sincerity and dedication to fostering real, meaningful change.

Scott Gleeson, counselor: Scott's faith, support, and friendship have been pivotal during my recovery. His wisdom, patience, and encouragement have provided strength and clarity during crucial moments. A man of Christ, Scott's devotion to King Jesus reminds us of His place in our lives. His unwavering faith and guidance have helped me navigate life's complexities with grace and conviction. Scott's dedication to living out Christ's teachings inspires all who know him, making his influence a cornerstone of my spiritual and personal growth.

John Henry Martin Burton, Jr., my grandfather: My greatest regret may be that I never had the opportunity to meet Grandfather Burton. Generations after his death, he is still teaching, leading, and nurturing, and I'm proud to be a part of his enduring legacy. Grandfather Burton, the patriarch of our family, whose strength, wisdom, and unwavering love have been the foundation of my life, taught me lessons in resilience, honor, and integrity. These principles are the bedrock upon which I stand. He instilled in me the value of hard work, the importance of family, the power of unconditional love, and the significance of unwavering faith. His deep faith in God was a guiding light, providing a moral compass and a source of strength in times of hardship. Grandfather, your legacy lives on in every step I take, and your memory is the ultimate honor that guides me through every challenge and triumph.

These men and women were placed in my life by God to challenge, encourage, inspire, and lift my heart. I believe He also put me in their lives to do the same. Their influence and support have been instrumental in shaping my journey, and I am profoundly grateful for their presence.

To those who've walked this path with me through these pages, I offer my deepest gratitude. Your willingness to witness my journey is a testament to the power of shared stories and the strength we find in one another. May you find in these words a spark of hope, a reminder of your resilience, and the courage to embrace your journey with faith and grace.

Let me encourage you to pray unceasingly and seek our Lord and Savior in all you do. Remember these words, inspired by the biblical imagery of Malachi 3:3 and 1 Peter 1:7:

> *Refine me, Lord, as gold is refined in the fire. Through every trial and challenge, may I emerge stronger, more faithful, and more attuned to Your will. Let my life be a testament to Your unfailing love and faithfulness. In Jesus' blessed name, Amen.*

In the sacred spaces of Belfast and Chartres, the tranquil beauty of Monet's Garden, the rugged trails of New Zealand, and the historic shipyards of Belfast, I've found reflections of my journey—resilience, faith, and the enduring quest for inner peace. These places and the stories of those who've walked before me inspire me to continue my journey with a renewed sense of purpose and hope. May we all find the strength to embrace the light, even in the midst of our shadows.

Beyond the Shadows

As I reflect on the journey that has brought me here, I'm struck by the profound lessons that have emerged from the shadows of my past. This memoir, a tapestry woven with threads of pain, resilience, and redemption, has illuminated truths that I once struggled to see. The path was never easy, but it was on this tumultuous journey that I discovered the most valuable lessons of my life.

The Pervasiveness of Fear and Violence

Growing up in an environment where fear and violence were the norms profoundly impacted my sense of safety and normalcy. My father's nightly returns, filled with physical and verbal abuse, created a constant atmosphere of fear. This fear became the backdrop of my childhood, leaving lasting scars that I've had to confront and understand.

Emotional Numbness and Insecurity

Prolonged exposure to trauma often leads to emotional numbness and deep-seated insecurity. Joyce Rachelle said it well: "Some scars don't hurt. Some scars are numb. Some scars rid you of the capacity to feel anything ever again." This resonates deeply with me. I spent much of my life alternating between feeling deeply insecure and utterly numb, using these as coping mechanisms to survive the turmoil.

The Loneliness of Deception

Deception, both self-imposed and toward others, becomes a defense mechanism that leads to profound isolation. I became an expert at hiding my true self, keeping people at a distance, and never letting anyone know the real me. This only deepened my loneliness and hindered my ability to form authentic connections.

The Burden of Responsibility

As children of alcoholics, we often take on adult responsibilities far too early, trying to mediate and manage family conflicts. I was the "responsible" child, trying to keep the peace during late-night arguments and maintaining calm. It was a heavy burden for someone so young, shaping my development and my approach to responsibilities in adulthood.

I became "the competent imposter" from the poem "Daughters of the Bottle." Like Jane, I likely spent much of my life hiding the turmoil and dysfunction caused by my father's alcoholism behind a facade of competence and leadership. I, too, perfected the art of the "stay-away smile," maintaining a professional exterior while internally grappling with the legacy of my family's struggles. My journey of seeking truth, understanding, and breaking the cycle of dysfunction mirrors the experiences of Jane and her peers, who also recognize and support each other in their shared struggles.

The Power of Faith and Resilience

Finding faith and spiritual peace can be a powerful source of resilience in the face of turmoil. During my darkest moments, my faith provided a profound sense of calm and assurance. It became a cornerstone of my resilience, helping me navigate the chaos. Faith, family, and a focus on health are my "Big Three"—in that order.

Long-Term Impact of Dysfunctional Upbringing

Growing up in a dysfunctional household leaves long-lasting effects, such as struggles with trust, emotional expression, and self-acceptance. The emotional scars and phantom memories continue to impact my relationships and self-perception even today.

The Cycle of Silence

Silence and secrecy are common in families dealing with alcoholism, perpetuating trauma and hindering healing. Our family lived by the unspoken rules of "Don't talk. Don't trust. Don't feel." This collective silence, especially among my siblings, exemplified this cycle and made breaking free from it even more challenging.

The Quest for Personal Identity

Finding personal identity amid the shadows of an alcoholic parent is a lifelong journey. Reflecting on the multiple roles I've played, overshadowed by being a child of an alcoholic, I realize the importance of embracing my true self and continuing my journey toward healing.

Steps to Healing

By reflecting on these questions, I believe readers can gain deeper insights into the lasting effects of growing up in an alcoholic household and take meaningful steps toward healing and personal growth. Remember, acknowledging and understanding your past is the first step to overcoming it and finding peace. If you are a child of an alcoholic, addressing the impact of your upbringing on your life can be challenging but deeply rewarding.

Here are some steps that may help you on your journey to healing and understanding:

1. **Acknowledge your experiences:** Recognize and validate your experiences and emotions. It's important to acknowledge the reality of your childhood and the impact it has had on your life.

2. **Seek professional help:** Consider finding a therapist or counselor who specializes in addiction and family dynamics. Professional guidance can provide you with the tools to understand and process your feelings.

3. **Join support groups:** Groups like Al-Anon or Adult Children of Alcoholics (ACoA) can offer support from others who have gone through similar experiences. Sharing your story and hearing others' can be incredibly validating and healing.

4. **Educate yourself:** Learn about the effects of growing up in an alcoholic household. Understanding the common patterns and behaviors can help you make sense of your experiences and recognize that you are not alone.

5. **Develop healthy coping mechanisms:** Find constructive ways to deal with stress and emotions. This might include walking in nature, exercise, meditation, journaling, or creative activities. Healthy coping strategies can replace any negative patterns you may have developed.

6. **Set boundaries:** Learning to set and maintain healthy boundaries is crucial. This applies not only to your relationship with the alcoholic parent but also in other areas of your life. Boundaries help protect your well-being and foster healthy relationships.

7. **Work on self-esteem:** Growing up with an alcoholic parent can negatively affect your self-esteem. Engage in activities that build your self-worth and surround yourself with supportive and positive people.

8. **Forgive yourself:** Understand that the coping mechanisms you developed as a child were necessary for your survival. Be gentle with yourself as you work through any feelings of guilt or shame.

9. **Forgive, but don't forget:** Forgiveness is a personal choice and can be an important step in healing. However, forgiveness does not mean excusing harmful behavior or forgetting the past. It's about freeing yourself from the burden of anger and resentment.

10. **Create a positive future:** Focus on building a life that is healthy, fulfilling, and free from the negative patterns of your past. Set goals, pursue your passions, and create a supportive network of friends and loved ones.

Recommended Books for Adult Children of Alcoholics

It Will Never Happen to Me: Growing Up with Addiction as Youngsters, Adolescents, and Adults and *Unspoken Legacy: Addressing the Impact of Trauma and Addiction within the Family* by Claudia Black, PhD

Both *It Will Never Happen to Me,* and *Unspoken Legacy* deeply resonate with my personal journey. In *It Will Never Happen to Me*, Claudia's exploration of childhood trauma helped me recognize how I had retreated into myself, projecting success while internally feeling numb and disconnected. In *Unspoken Legacy*, her focus on the lasting impact of trauma and addiction within families provided further clarity, showing me how generational trauma shapes every aspect of life. Together, these books gave me the tools to confront my past, unmask buried pain, and move forward with forgiveness, gratitude, and self-love.

Healing Your Lost Inner Child: How to Stop Impulsive Reactions, Set Healthy Boundaries and Embrace an Authentic Life and *Healing Your Lost Inner Child Companion Workbook* by Robert Jackman, MS, LCPC, NCC

Robert has been a wonderful friend and guide throughout my journey. His book *Healing Your Lost Inner Child* offers a profound exploration of the emotional wounds that adult children of alcoholics often carry, while the *Healing Your Lost Inner Child Companion Workbook* provides practical tools to further engage in the healing process. Together, these books have been invaluable, not only in my own recovery but for countless others seeking healing and peace.

Adult Children of Alcoholics by Janet G. Woititz

This classic book offers a comprehensive look at the common characteristics and struggles faced by adult children of alcoholics. It provides insights and strategies for understanding and overcoming the long-term effects of growing up in an alcoholic household.

Perfect Daughters: Adult Daughters of Alcoholics by Robert J. Ackerman

Focusing on the unique experiences of daughters of alcoholics, this book delves into the specific challenges they face. It offers guidance on breaking free from dysfunctional patterns and building healthier relationships.

Afterword

As water reflects the face, so one's life reflects the heart.
—Proverbs 27:19

This verse has always held a profound meaning for me, but it has taken on even greater significance in light of my journey through healing and self-discovery.

Just as water provides an unaltered reflection of our physical appearance, our actions, and choices are a true reflection of our inner selves—our hearts. This journey has taught me that what we project into the world is a direct mirror of our internal state. When my heart was burdened with unresolved trauma, pain, and fear, my life reflected chaos, anxiety, and a sense of helplessness.

Through therapy and introspection, I began to heal those deep wounds. As my heart became lighter, filled with understanding and self-compassion, my life began to reflect peace, strength, and resilience. This proverb reminds me that the work we do internally is essential to the lives we lead externally. It is a call to continuously nurture and heal our hearts, knowing that this will be mirrored in the quality of our lives.

Healing is a journey, and it's okay to take it one step at a time. Your past does not define you; you have the power to create a positive and fulfilling future. Remember, the path to healing begins with the first step of acknowledging your experiences. By embracing your past and seeking support, you can break free from the shadows and build a life filled with hope, resilience, and purpose.

And now, as I bring this memoir to a close, I find myself reflecting deeply: Whatever happened to the boy I once was? Where did he go? What happened to his dreams? He's still here, but now he's integrated fully into the man I am as a result of my healing.

Free of judgment, full of understanding, I embrace the totality of my experiences, recognizing that the journey is as important as the destination. The memories never fade, and I can still feel them as I once lived those experiences. The sadness and loss remain as poignant today as they were then.

As I close the final chapter, I find myself overwhelmed with a flood of emotions. The act of revisiting my life, of laying bare my struggles, my fears, and my triumphs, has been both cathartic and heart-wrenching. There were moments when the pain of my past felt as vivid as it did decades ago, and others when the resilience and strength I discovered within myself brought tears of gratitude and relief.

Writing this memoir has been an exercise in vulnerability. It's like peeling back the layers of scar tissue to expose the wounds that have long since healed but left their mark. The tears I shed now are not just for the sorrow of what was endured but also for the immense relief of having finally given voice to my story. They are tears of release, of letting go of the shadows that have loomed over me, and embracing the light that has always been within reach.

In this process, I'm reminded of a quote by novelist Salman Rushdie: "Those who do not have power over the story that dominates their lives, power to retell it, to rethink it, deconstruct it, joke about it, and change it as times change, truly are powerless." His message resonates deeply with me. By retelling my story—by deconstructing and reshaping it—I've reclaimed the power that once seemed lost. This memoir goes beyond recounting my past; it embodies the strength I've gained and the transformation I've undergone through the act of storytelling.

In sharing my journey, I hope to connect with others who have faced similar battles, to let them know they are not alone, and to offer a glimmer of hope. If my experiences can help even one person find their way out of the darkness, then every tear, every painful memory, and every moment of doubt will have been worth it.

My memoir is a testament to the past and lights the path for my future—a future where the lessons learned and the strength gained continue to guide me. As I wipe away the last of these tears, I'm reminded of the power of resilience, the importance of faith, and the incredible journey of self-discovery that life offers us all. The truth of Proverbs 27:19 is evident in every step of this journey. It encourages me to maintain a heart full of love, empathy, and resilience, knowing that this will be reflected in the life I continue to build.

As you embark on your own journey, may you find the strength to embrace your story, the courage to seek healing, and the faith to believe in a brighter tomorrow. Each step you take is a testament to your resilience and a promise of the light that lies ahead.

Acknowledgments

To my beloved children—Jarrett, Jordan, and Tyler—even in my darkest times, when impatience, anger, and resentment clouded my heart, you couldn't fully understand the reasons behind my struggles, nor were you ever the cause. Yet, you stood by me with love and support. Thank you for your patience and for always welcoming me with open hearts. You have been a source of strength and hope for me, and for that, I am deeply grateful.

To my grandchildren, for whom I hope this book serves as a guide and testament to our family's resilience.

To our neighboring families on Rock Creek Drive in Garland, Texas, whose lives I admired and secretly longed to join in search of normalcy—thank you for providing a beacon of hope to the little boy who watched how you lived your lives.

To the teachers, coaches, classmates, pastors, mentors, counselors, friends, and colleagues who have offered steadfast guidance and support—you will forever be in my thoughts and prayers.

To David Aretha, who has authored and edited hundreds of great books, thank you for your wise counsel and guidance as my editor.

To Martha Bullen of Bullen Publishing Services—your deep knowledge, experience, instincts, and judgment are invaluable, consistently elevating my work with keen insights and thoughtful suggestions. You helped me create the path for my memoir when I most needed a trusted guide and partner on my journey. As I've told you, we were always meant to work together!

To Christy Day of Constellation Book Services, you have my heartfelt thanks for the incredible cover design for *Shadows of Sobriety* and the expert layout of the book. Your creativity, vision, and ability to bring the visual concepts of my memoir to life were truly inspiring.

And to anyone who has felt the weight of their past bearing down on their present, yet dares to believe in the possibility of a brighter future, stay the course.

About the Author

Keith Burton is an award-winning public relations leader, journalist, and co-producer of the acclaimed documentary *Dax's Case*, which explores ethical dilemmas and patient autonomy regarding the right to die. He is the founder of Grayson Emmett Partners, LLC.

With over four decades of experience in communications and leading major public relations agencies, Keith is recognized as an authority on engaging front-line leaders and hourly employees, aligning the workforce with business strategies, driving corporate culture in the age of the hybrid model, and developing leadership skills for communications teams. Throughout his illustrious career, he has worked with *Fortune 500* companies worldwide.

Keith lectures on leadership and communications at colleges and universities throughout the United States and serves as a member of the PR Practitioners Advisory Group at the S.I. Newhouse School of Public Communications at Syracuse University. He also serves on the board of the annual International Public Relations Research Conference (IPRRC). Keith is deeply committed to mentoring educators and the next generation of leaders in public relations. He is an emeritus board member and past chair of The Plank Center for Leadership in Public

Relations. He actively participates in various industry conferences and workshops, sharing his expertise and fostering the growth of upcoming professionals.

Additionally, Keith is dedicated to community service, volunteering his time to support local initiatives that address addiction recovery. His ongoing contributions to thought leadership in public relations and his unwavering support for ethical practices in journalism and corporate communication underscore his commitment to making a meaningful impact both professionally and personally.

Keith's memoir, *Shadows of Sobriety*, delves into his family's struggles with alcoholism, his own battles with panic attacks, and the impact of his parents' behavior on his childhood and adult life. The memoir explores themes of resilience, faith, and the pursuit of redemption.

He lives in the Chicago area with his wife and two golden retrievers. They have three children and five grandchildren who also live in the area. To learn more or contact Keith, visit www.shadowsofsobriety.com.

Printed in Great Britain
by Amazon

59246670R00116